SHATTERED Innocence

Healing the Invisible Wounds of Childhood Trauma

GRAHAM ROBINSON

HILLE HOUSE PUBLISHING

Copyright © 2025, Graham Robinson. All rights reserved.

No part of this publication may be reproduced, stored in a retrieval system, or transmitted in any form or by any means without prior written permission from the publisher, apart from any use permitted under the *Copyright Act 1968* and subsequent amendments. The stories in this book reflect the author's recollection of events. Some names, locations, and identifying characteristics have been changed to protect the privacy of those depicted. Dialogue has been re-created from memory.

Cover Design © Dragoslav Andjelkovic

Original Cover Design © Canva Creative Studio

Interior Design © Hille House Publishing

Author's photo © Olivia Leigh Photography

Published © Hille House Publishing

First edition © 2025

Print ISBN: 978-0-6457854-3-2

Ebook ISBN: 978-0-6457854-4-9

Audiobook ISBN: 978-0-6457854-5-6

A catalogue record for this work is available from the National Library of Australia

Dedication

This book is dedicated to my three beautiful children: Jessica, Kyan and Kaleb.

A child is a butterfly in the wind.
Some can fly higher than others.
Why compare one against the other?
Each one flies the best it can.
Each one is different!
Each one is special!
Each one is beautiful!
—Author unknown

Contents

Introduction   VIII
- The Wounded Inner Child
- Adult Inner Child
- Healing Journey

Chapter One: Original Wound   1
- Reflection: Adverse Childhood Experiences
- Adult Reaction: Unworthy
- Healing Exercise: Meeting the Inner Child

Chapter Two: Echoes of Fear   10
- Reflection: Bully or Bullied?
- Adult Reaction: Survival
- Healing Exercise: Behaviour Correction

Chapter Three: Hiding in Plain Sight   18
- Reflection: Fawning Behaviour
- Adult Reaction: Standing Up
- Healing Exercise: Butterfly Hug

Chapter Four: Illusion Care   27
- Reflection: Codependency
- Adult Reaction: Risky Behaviour
- Healing Exercise: Being Still

Chapter Five: Whispers in the Dark — 38
- Reflection: Toxic Shame
- Adult Reaction: Deserving Better
- Healing Exercise: Emotional Recovery

Chapter Six: Edge of Collapse — 47
- Reflection: Intergenerational Trauma
- Adult Reaction: Parent Trauma
- Healing Exercise: Revisiting the Past

Chapter Seven: Road to Nowhere — 57
- Reflection: The Father Wound
- Adult Reaction: Absent Father
- Healing Exercise: Letter Writing

Chapter Eight: Walking on Eggshells — 67
- Reflection: People-Pleasing
- Adult Reaction: Connection
- Healing Exercise: Validating Ourselves

Chapter Nine: Silent Goodbye — 80
- Reflection: Abandonment
- Adult Reaction: Sex Addiction
- Healing Exercise: Embracing Vulnerability

Chapter Ten: Echoes of Childhood — 92
- Reflection: Complex Trauma
- Adult Reaction: Rage
- Healing Exercise: Calming Therapy

Chapter Eleven: Rebelling Against Control — 103
- Reflection: Authority Wound
- Adult Reaction: Monster Within
- Healing Exercise: Becoming You

Chapter Twelve: Burden of Blame   118
- Reflection: Guilt
- Adult Reaction: Needing Love
- Healing Exercise: Forgiving

Chapter Thirteen: Shadow of Fear   126
- Reflection: Fear
- Adult Reaction: Repressed Trauma
- Healing Exercise: Breathwork

Chapter Fourteen: Dance of Doubt   143
- Reflection: Insecure Attachments
- Adult Reaction: Loneliness
- Healing Exercise: Being Present

Chapter Fifteen: Brave Heart   157
- Reflection: Resilience
- Adult Reaction: Being Alone
- Healing Exercise: Valuing Ourselves

Chapter Sixteen: Close but Distant   165
- Reflection: Intimacy
- Adult Reaction: Perfection
- Healing Exercise: Nurturing

Chapter Seventeen: Facing the Abyss   178
- Reflection: Self-Destruction
- Adult Reaction: Hopelessness
- Healing Exercise: Acceptance

Chapter Eighteen: Lost Connection   188
- Reflection: Attachment Disorder
- Adult Reaction: Emotional Neglect
- Healing Exercise: Visualisation

Chapter Nineteen: Unspoken Truth   198
- Reflection: Anger
- Adult Reaction: Childish Behaviour
- Healing Exercise: Forgiveness

Chapter Twenty: Silent Rage   211
- Reflection: The Authentic Self
- Adult Reaction: It's Never Too Late
- Healing Exercise: Ho'oponopono Prayer

About the Author   223
Acknowledgements   224
Resources   225

Introduction

"Our inner child can drive many of our emotions in our daily life, especially when we are unaware of it. When you lose conscious awareness of your inner child, you lose conscious awareness of a part of yourself."

— Carl Jung

The Wounded Inner Child

Have you ever felt a deep sadness you couldn't explain? Or reacted in anger without knowing why? Perhaps you struggle with self-worth or think that you don't belong in this world. These are all elements of a wounded inner child, and they stem from childhood trauma.

Suppose your caregiver (this includes parents and all non-biological carers) loved and cared for you, showed appropriate boundaries, and helped build healthy relationships. Then you are one of the lucky ones. Every day, you should thank them for being who they are. For the rest of us who suffered childhood abuse, it's heartbreaking.

Our childhood was locked away, our true feelings and emotions hidden. Because of the abuse, we created an alternative reality, one filled with false dreams, hopes, and desires. A made-up person to make everyone around us happy and love us. Did it work? No. What it does do is leave us with deep emotional trauma.

As we grow into adults, these emotional traumas manifest and drive our responses. Many will think they know us, but only we know our true struggle below the surface.

A key factor in our trauma is how and if it's processed. Some can experience traumatic events with minimal lasting adverse effects, while many will carry the trauma into adulthood.

Across the globe, one in four adults report childhood physical abuse and one in eight report sexual abuse. These are not just statistics but experiences of survivors. Many remain haunted by their early childhood abuse without realising it. People over seventy kill themselves at nearly three times the rate of the general population. When caregivers abuse us, it's their issue, not ours. But, as children, we feel responsible. We think we are flawed or imperfect in some way. It's the beginning of life with a wounded inner child.

Adult Inner Child

This book is not a clinical examination of early childhood trauma; it's a lived experience and a survivor's story. Each chapter shares a part of my early childhood and reflects on my adult trauma experience. Together we'll explore the impact of shame, guilt, anger, self-loathing, low self-esteem and the inability to have healthy relationships.

I'll share my rage-filled childhood up to the time I left home at thirteen and the painful experiences that followed. I'll explain the individual traumas and the emotional responses as an adult.

I was born in 1956. Five years later, I was a sad, angry, and lonely child. I didn't appreciate the damage childhood abuse had waged on me until I was in my fifties. It was then that I broke down sobbing when I saw a father on television place an arm around his son's shoulders. I realised I had a problem. Until then, I'd ignored the signs: a violent temper, inability to connect with people, a need to please everyone and my shame.

Not all child abuse has to be physical or sexual to have an impact. Emotional abuse, such as an unkind word, constant criticism, or repetitive shaming, also has a significant effect. But sexual abuse is by far the worst.

One of the lasting effects of childhood abuse is the feeling of not being able to connect with others, even family. Mourners surrounded me at my father's funeral. I listened to my brother's trembling voice as he eulogised my father. I wanted to comfort him, but I remained motionless. I didn't recognise my father in his words. My heart didn't ache. Tears didn't spill. In its place was an emptiness. It's one of the effects of childhood trauma — a wound so deep that even when we should grieve, we feel nothing.

Healing Journey

As a survivor of childhood abuse, I want to accompany you on your healing journey. I'll provide resources to help you connect with your inner child and to manage your emotional trauma. Use what feels right. If it doesn't, then choose something else: we all have different paths in our healing journey. Healing isn't quick, and setbacks happen, but we'll navigate those together. However, this book does not replace the need for professional therapy. Mine began with *Emotion-focused treatment (EFT)*, or tapping as it's known. It paved the way for more intense healing with the *Australian Chapter of Path Retreats*. During one of their retreats, I had to imagine entering a dark cave to find the source of my pain. Before stepping into this imaginary cave, I looked back and, in my mind's eye, saw thousands of children standing on each other's shoulders. They covered mountains and filled valleys. To me, they symbolised every child who was suffering from childhood trauma. It brought me to tears.

I encourage you to reflect on your trauma reactions, both good and bad. And the impact they have on your life? Self-reflection is essential; it helps change our negative emotions into positive ones. As we travel this path, we may scream or cry. I've done both, but relief arrives. Remember, we are responsible for our healing.

Before diving into this book, give yourself credit for coming as far as you have and for surviving. That isn't easy. Our childhood trauma is complex and creates multiple challenges for us as adults. But it shouldn't continue to shape our lives. Know that we have the power to reimagine our future. My vision is for a world where survivors of childhood abuse live happy, healthy, emotionally balanced lives. Let me start by sharing my story.

Chapter One

Original Wound

Legs, skinny and tanned, and others pale with red spots. The parade passed, laughter and chatter filling the air, all oblivious to you crouched in front of the shop. Your fingers brush the cool metal of the toy helicopter. Its body gleamed, and the tiny blades caught the light as they whirred. A thrill ran through you. Without thinking, two slip into your pocket.

***

His arm lay across the bench seat. Hand clenching and unclenching. He stares. You've felt this before — the weight of something inevitable.

'Where did you get 'em? Answer me, or I swear...'

His voice is low and edgy. Your mother stares straight ahead with no indication she's heard. Your fingers curl around the helicopters, the joy replaced with a sick dread.

'Get out.'

Your stomach plunges. Hesitating, looking at your brother. His eyes are sad as they meet yours, but he doesn't move. Clumsily, you scramble over his knees, your heart pounding as the door opens. Your father unhooks his belt.

You run.

Ferns crack beneath your feet, the undergrowth tearing at your legs as you seek a hiding place. The sharp scent of pine fills your nose, mingling with your fear.

Behind you, heavy footfalls signal he's close. You sink to the ground in defeat, back pressed against the rough bark of a pine tree — your breath is shallow. You wish you were small enough to disappear. A shadow falls over you.

Staring at his loafers, as he calls them. Grains of sand still cling to them from the beach. Ignoring the dampness in your pants, you fix your eyes on a frayed lace. *Does he know? Maybe tell him?* Your heart races, quickly pushing the thought away.

His mouth moves, but the words blur, lost in the roaring in your ears. Gripping the helicopters, tiny, fragile things that had meant so much.

Your eyes lift, not to his face, to the belt dangling at his side, its worn leather coiled like a snake.

His hand shot out, fingers clamping around your arm, yanking you to your feet. His grip bruising as he drags you back to the car, shoving you to the ground.

The damp earth soaks into your plimsolls — a recent fifth birthday present — now turning brown. You want to speak to make this stop. But it won't matter. It never did. You don't answer.

The taste of the afternoon's chocolate ice cream sours in your throat. The passing parade of cars ignoring the idling Zodiac and the man with his son.

His eyes darkened as he held out his hand. Hesitating, a glance at the car — your mother hasn't moved. Your brother can't meet your eyes. There's no escape.

Hand shaking, you place the helicopters into his palm. They sit there, shining brightly. Then — *CRUNCH*. He grinds them into the earth, tiny pieces buried in the dirt.

'You can't just take whatever you want.' A vein pulses in his neck. 'You asked for this.'

Pain explodes in your left ear, sharp and searing. Hands flying to your face, fingers come away wet with blood.

Another. Then another. *Thwack — thwack — thwack.*

You curl into a ball, fists clenched, swallowing the cries. The blows keep coming, driving the air from your lungs.

With a ragged breath, he gasps, 'Get... get back in the car.'

Your body aches with every movement as you slide onto the red leather seat, searching for a position that doesn't hurt. The engine roars and the car lurches forward.

Your brother stares straight ahead, too afraid to speak.

Your burning cheek is pressed to the window, letting the cool glass numb the stinging. Outside, butterflies dance above the cow parsley, weightless, free.

Your eyes drift to the rear view mirror. His gaze meets yours. Cold. Empty. Unblinking.

Something new settles in your chest. A forlorn hope that has now turned to fear. One day, you'll understand.

***

Snow blankets the railway station, soft and untouched from the previous night's fall. The crisp morning air bites at your cheeks. The sharp whistle of the train startles the gathered crowd. Your father is standing in the centre, shaking hands and nodding at words you couldn't hear.

You watch from the carriage steps — curiosity mingled with something else. You pull your jacket tighter, but the cold seeps in. On the platform, a guard in a royal-blue coat marched back and forth, his red-striped trousers stiff with starch. He waves a green flag. 'All aboard!'

Your father's friends unfurl a bedsheet, its uneven letters declaring: Good luck in Africa, Robinsons.

The train shuddered, then lurched forward. King's Lynn blurs through the window into a smear of white fields.

Closing your yes and letting the rhythmic clack-clack of the wheels lull you to sleep. Dreams of lions and elephants prowling through thick jungle and adventures fill your head. Africa, for you, is a place that exists on the pages of National Geographic.

***

The customs shed is a different world — sweltering, stifling, thick with the scent of sweat and spoiled food. The heat clung to you, sinking into your bones. Excitement drained in the sapping humidity.

Men in uniform speak in clipped voices, their eyes darting between papers and your father. The back of his neck was red, glowing with barely contained frustration. You knew that colour well. Holding your breath, you wait. Nothing had changed with him. This week's events proved that.

***

A crowd pressed around the ship's pool, a carnival of laughter and the slap of feet on the deck. A man dressed as Neptune — with an emerald waistcoat shimmering, brandished a yellow trident above his head. You recognise him. He cleans your cabin.

'The pool is now open,' he announces.

You shove forward with the other children, eager to claim a spot. The sun glares off the water as you bend your knees, tucking in your legs as you jump in — the ship tilts, the pool water sloshes, and then — a sharp crack against your skull. Water surges back, swallowing you.

Panic grips you. Kicking. Thrashing. Your world is reduced to a desperate need for air. Strong hands drag you onto the pool's edge, coughing, heaving. Water pours from your mouth.

Someone drapes a wet towel over your shoulders. A stranger murmurs something about taking you to your cabin. You shiver.

Your father walks ahead, stiff-backed, his silence louder than words.

Your mother's voice, a whisper: 'Keep walking.'

You stand in the centre of the room. Your mother's arms folded, her face unreadable. Water drips from your hair, darkening the carpet, pressing your lips together, telling yourself not to cry. Slowly, you turn to your father.

His face is a blank mask.

Reaching for the towel, he slips it off your shoulders and twists it in his hands until it resembles a braided length of rope. Your legs buckle. With a flick of his wrist, the first strike lands.

Desperate to escape, scrambling to the corner of the bottom bunk. A plea in your throat. The towel snaps again.

Your mother's hand brushes his arm. He shoves it away, not looking at her.

'You always embarrass us.' His voice was low, seething. 'You can stay here for the rest of the day.'

The door clicks shut.

Sliding from the bunk, you curl up on the thin nylon carpet. Its solid, unmoving firmness comforts you. You try to remember a time when he cared about you.

You had felt pride once and thought he did. It was the day the school announced you'd won third place in the art competition with a drawing of the Beatles. You stood at the back of the hall, watching other children bask in their families' joy. No one came for you. At that moment, you understood. Later, you threw the award away. Sitting up. The memory is cold inside you. There are no more tears.

Reflection: Adverse Childhood Experiences

"People with rational adult lives may continue to live stormy emotional lives. Their storms persist because they haven't addressed their initial pain." — John Bradshaw

The abuse we suffered as children means we suppress our feelings leaving us with deep-seated emotional trauma. Because our abuse happens at a young age, we're not able to escape the trauma and our nervous system remains on constant alert. This leads to us remaining in a constant state of fear. We detach from the reality around us as it is too painful to not be loved. We also lose our trust. How can we trust anyone if the people we love abuse us.

As children, we learn from the actions of our carers even when bad or abusive. The son watching an alcoholic father beat his mother often repeats that scene in his own relationships.

Why? Because it's familiar and what our inner child feels comfortable with. That may be difficult to understand, being comfortable with violence. But the fearful inner child has learnt this model of behaviour, so to it, this must be the right one.

To understand childhood abuse we must acknowledge what happened to us. One of the most effective tools for doing this is the Adverse Childhood Experiences (ACEs) questionnaire — it's a series of questions designed to understand the impact of early childhood abuse. The higher the ACE score, the more significant the childhood trauma. But it's important to remember that ACEs don't define us or determine our future. Calculate your number of ACE experiences from the following ten questions:

- Did you experience anything that caused you intentional physical harm?

- Did you experience any unwanted or abusive sexual behaviour?

- Did you experience anything that caused emotional harm, such as bullying, being unloved or being made to feel guilty?

- Did your caregivers fail to meet your basic food, water, and shelter needs?

- Did your caregivers fail to provide for your emotional needs, such as love, attention, and affection?

- Did you experience violence or constant shouting between your caregivers or other family members?

- Did any family member misuse drugs or alcohol?

- Did any family member or significant person in your life experience mental health problems?

- Has any family member or significant person in your life been in prison?

- Did your caregivers separate or divorce due to a relationship breakdown?

I had three ACEs. I thought this was low, considering the trauma I experienced as a child and continued to experience as an adult. However, ACEs do not work in isolation. They're cumulative. A single ACE can have a lifelong effect.

Another consequence of ACEs is the risk of chronic health problems. The University College of London released a study that indicated that if we have two or *more ACEs, we are more susceptible to developing Cancers, liver disease, diabetes or strokes. To learn more about the health impacts of ACEs, watch Nadine Burke Harris's TED talk,* How Childhood Trauma Affects Health Across a Lifetime, *or read her book,* The Deepest Well: Healing the Long-Term Effects of Childhood Adversity.

Adult Reaction: Unworthy

Our childhood wounds shape our adult responses in ways that are difficult to comprehend or control. Mine, at times, have been extreme. They first surfaced at eighteen following an incident with my girlfriend after Cyclone Tracy hit Darwin in 1974. My parent's and sisters came to stay with me in Sydney following the Cyclone. One day, my girlfriend approached me, upset that my mother had rearranged the furniture in the house. My reaction was to hurl the plate I was holding onto the floor, shattering it into small fragments and grabbing her by the neck, lifting her off the ground. Fortunately, I regained my senses and released her. As she ran from the kitchen, I couldn't forget the horrified expression on her face. I felt sick and ashamed, unable to understand why I'd reacted like that. My only explanation is that criticising my mother triggered long held fears in my inner child. These were the fears of not being loved by her and therefore needing to do everything to please her. I needed to stop the criticism to feel safe and believe I would be loved.

Always keep in mind it is the emotional inner child reacting not the logical adult.

Much of our negative emotional responses are linked to these deep seated feelings of being unworthy and unloved. Have you had a similar reaction when either parent has been criticised by a partner? If so, think about your reaction and how you can change.

Healing Exercise: Meeting the Inner Child

The wounds from childhood abuse don't simply disappear — they become fear and survival-driven behaviours. No matter how deep, healing is possible. Understanding that our past abuse is defining our present behaviour is the first step.

The most essential ingredient in healing the inner child is love. And to provide this, we have to reparent the child within. This involves stepping into the role of a supportive and loving caregiver providing the care and support it didn't receive in childhood. As you progress through this book, remind yourself that you are the caregiver for your inner child. If this feels strange, then you're not alone. It did for me, too. But I came to realise the power of reparenting and the joy it brought me.

Let me explain how we do this. First we will meet our inner child. To begin, get comfortable, either seated or lying down. Close your eyes and breathe deeply for a few minutes. Breathe in through your nose, then slowly release through your mouth. Starting at the top of your head, feel a wave of relaxation moving down your body. Move this relaxing energy down to the tips of your toes.

Now, take your time and imagine walking through a peaceful and relaxing forest. You see a small figure walking towards you. The figure moves cautiously. As it gets closer, you recognise your inner child. Sit down with them and ask how they are feeling. Be patient. Take your time, and wait for a reply. Ask what they need from you. Explain what you've learned from adulthood.

Remember, we understand and see things differently as adults than we did as children. Tell your inner child that their parents did their best with what they had. Promise your inner child that you will do everything you can to give it what it needs. From now on, you'll be here for it. Tell them this and mean it. Then give your inner child a big hug and tell it you love it. Hold it close and feel the love between you. Now, imagine holding a gold cape. It glows and shimmies with a golden hue. It's a magical cape. Wrap this cape around its shoulders. The cape symbolises the protection and love you are offering. As you do this, it fades away, becoming one with you again. Finally, take a deep breath and open your eyes. Congratulations.

You have begun the first step of healing. I recommend journaling any thoughts you had from this exercise.

Therapy, inner child work and self-compassion all help us change our childhood belief that we are unworthy or flawed. It's important that you take care of yourself, practice self-care through meditation and spend time in nature, as this will calm your emotional wounds. Remember, others don't define our worth. We do. Never forget this.

The abuse I endured at the hands of my father shattered my sense of self-worth, but the deeper wound was the feeling of being unloved. That wouldn't fade. Unknowingly, I invited others to treat me the way he did, as if I had no right to expect any better. In the next chapter, I'll explore why.

Chapter Two

Echoes of Fear

'Your name?' The woman behind the counter asks, peering over glasses perched on a thin nose. It reminds you of a bird's beak; you smile at the thought until a sharp look from her wipes it away.

'Well? What is it?'

Your first day at Darwin High is not going well.

'Um, it's Robinson... Miss.' You drop your head, staring at your shoes as if something fascinating is happening to them.

She exhales, placing the paper she's holding onto the counter. The fan rattles, sending the sheet fluttering in the breeze.

'Your full name?' A trace of impatience in her voice.

'Oh. It's Graham. Graham Robinson.'

'Graham, Graham Robinson,' she repeats flatly. No smile. Turning her back, she snatches a clipboard from a peg, scanning its attached page with a dismissive tut. 'You're not on the list, Graham, Graham Robinson.' A flicker at the corner of her mouth. The clipboard returns to its peg with an irritated snap. She smooths her already crisply pleated skirt. Frowns. 'How old are you? Do you know your teacher's name?'

You shake your head. 'No. I'm, um, twelve.'

'Hmm.' A pause. 'Go to classroom four. Tell the teacher it's your first day. They'll sort it out.'

The phone rings, and she picks it up, waving you away as if you've already ceased to exist. The thought of turning around and going home crosses your mind — but you can't. You're in trouble there, too, for spilling milk in the fridge. *As if it was my fault.*

A snicker draws your attention. A boy sits beside a door with 'PRINCIPAL' etched on its glass pane. He's smirking, like the woman, covers the mouthpiece with her hand, and who levels a glare at him. 'Quiet, Mr. Edwards. You're already in sufficient trouble.'

His eyes narrow. He mouths, 'Watch yourself, Graham, Graham Robinson.'

Outside, an open window offers a glimpse into a classroom. A male voice recites names, each one met with a murmur of acknowledgment. You hesitate between finding your classroom and dreading interrupting a lesson.

A lone figure sits on a bench, flicking stones across the cracked, bitumen-patched playground. Maybe he knows where the classroom is. You approach. 'Hey, do you know where classroom four is?'

He glances up, one eyebrow raised. 'Over there, I think.' A vague gesture toward the empty playing fields. He picks up another pebble, flicking it effortlessly against a wall.

'Why aren't you in class?'

A grin spreads across his face. 'Don't like school.'

You smile, stooping to pick up a stone, trying to mimic his throw. It bounces once, then stops. He laughs.

'I'm Larry. You new here?'

You nod, telling him about the woman at the counter and the boy near the principal's office.

Larry's expression darkens. 'Ah, Edwards. Yeah, he's a prick. His old man's important, so he acts like he is, too. Stay away from him.' His voice was stern.

The school bell shrills, shattering the moment and sending a jolt of panic through you. 'I should find my classroom.'

Larry shrugs, unconcerned. 'I'm going into town.'

Students spill out of the grey block building, flooding the stairwell. Among them, Edwards stands tall, imposing. You sling your bag over your shoulder, hoping to go unnoticed, then take off after Larry.

***

The click of playing cards in bicycle spokes sends a chill through you. They'd been at Parap shops, like you.

You clutch the comics to your chest, a Violet Crumble melting in your other hand. A brief thought of running would only delay the inevitable. With a sigh, you brace yourself.

Edwards pedals past, skidding his bike to block your path. 'What you doing here, Robinson? On my street?'

'It's not your street.'

His head jerks. 'Wadda, you say?' He drops his bike, dust puffs around his feet.

You haven't been this close to him since the principal's office. He's gangly, all awkward limbs — freckles on his long, scowling face. The top of your head barely reaches his chin. You're both skinny, but older people say you have lovely blue eyes. They mean nothing to Edwards.

'Hey! I'm talking to you, Robinson.'

A red-haired boy pulls up, wheezing. 'Yeah, Robinson. He's talking to you.'

'Shut up, Harold.'

Harold pulls a face but says nothing more. Edwards steps closer.

'What's in your hand?' He snatches the comics. Scoffs. 'Comics? What a baby.'

Harold squeaks as his bike wobbles, toppling him over. He bounces up, brushing the dirt off his pants. 'He's a baby! You tell him!'

Edwards rolls his eyes.

Fear slithers in you, but you push it aside. 'They're mine. Give 'em back.'

Edwards ignores you, flipping through the pages. 'Archie? What a sissy.' He flings it into the air. The wind snatches it, tumbling it down the street.

He holds onto the real prize: the new Fantastic Four. The reason you went to the shops.

Your eyes drop to the ground.

Edwards steps closer. He smells like gym class. Liniment and sweat. 'Gonna do something about it?' His fist strikes your chest, pushing you backward into Harold. Hands grip your shoulders, driving you forward again.

He sneers. 'Wanna fight, Robinson?' Edward's eyes glint. His fist slams into your stomach, knocking the breath from you.

'Better stay out of my way, or you'll get more.'

The click of bicycle spokes fades. Harold's parting words ringing in your ears: 'Do what he says, or else.'

Your head spins — thoughts of revenge simmer. But deep down, another truth takes root.

You believe you deserve this. After all, it's happened before.

***

Mr. Hendriks was the woodwork teacher at a school in Windhoek, a haven for Boer families. They boarded their children there during the week and returned to their farms on weekends. Harry and Cecil were the worst of them. They hated you. But their hate was nothing compared to Mr. Hendriks' malice.

Bawling in Afrikaans, he pointed. 'Antwoord die vraag.'

You didn't understand Afrikaans.

'What's wrong? You stupid? Speak up, boy!' Laughter rippled through the classroom.

'Stop that. Come here.'

You hesitate.

'Now.'

You shuffle forward.

'What? What did you say? I can't hear you.'

'Yes, sir.'

'Goed.' He repeated the question. Your mind is blank as you stare at the sea of unfriendly faces.

'You not answer?' His roar makes you jump.

'I don't... I don't understand Afrikaans, Sir.'

Silence. No pity in the eyes looking back at you. 'If you live here, you learn our language. Ja?'

His thick fingers, rough from years of woodwork, pinch the skin inside your thigh. Twisting.

You grit your teeth. Desperate not to cry out.

'Let us try again, ja?'

Same response from you. The twisting deeper.

'Stupid English boy. Go back to your seat.'

Limping to your desk, skin darkening to blue, you dread recess.

Reflection: Bully or Bullied?

"No one heals himself by wounding another." — St. Ambrose

For a child struggling with rejection, shame or inadequacy, bullying is more than just a painful experience — it reinforces the belief of being unworthy. My home environment taught me that power equals control. My father was a bully and I mirrored his tactics for self-protection. At times, I became a bully too, because I saw it as the only way to have power and control. But, that illusion of control kept me trapped in a trauma I was trying to escape. It is also misguided, as we often feel ashamed of our behaviour. Unfortunately, these conflicting emotions can lead to more bullying as we try to overcome the feeling of shame for our actions. This vicious cycle will continue until we understand that it is our early childhood trauma driving these reactions.

Not all of us become bullies. Instead, some may adopt a response based on survival by avoiding eye contact for fear of being a target, acting distant or unaffected. We might also disassociate from what is happening even when physically assaulted. No matter how we respond, the impact of bullying mixed with our past trauma is severe.

Adult Reaction: Survival

Every bully I encountered appeared to sense my lack of self-worth. Their blows had a longer-lasting effect on my emotional state than they did on me physically. It reinforced my belief that I was worthless. My response was to become the bully.

It surfaced whenever I had authority over others. I know now I was attempting to replicate the power and control my father had over me. It became so bad that on one occasion, I threatened a co-worker with physical violence. He'd made a mistake, and in my rage, I threatened to break his leg if he did it again. I was aware he felt bullied and traumatised. Looking back, I recognise that this was a shameful incident.

My bullying behaviour continued; it was as if I was trying to compensate for all of the pain from my childhood. As a manager, I would berate staff and insist they do everything my way. Eventually, they rebelled, and my behaviour cost me my job. Even then, I failed to recognise that I was a bully. I justified my actions by claiming they were necessary, and it wasn't my fault.

Reflecting on those times, I am horrified that I wasn't more self-aware. I always had an excuse. I understand now that my inner child felt safer being the aggressor than the victim. It's important we recognise and acknowledge our poor behaviour, no matter how difficult it is. If we don't, we will face self-doubt, self-sabotage, an inability to connect in relationships and people-pleasing tendencies. We must identify and resolve these conflicts within us, or we'll continue to damage all those who come into contact with us.

Healing Exercise: Behaviour Correction

Self-reflection is a powerful tool for understanding how bullying has affected us. We should also share our feelings with someone we trust. They can help us see our worth and build our confidence. If you don't have someone like this, seek a professional therapist to assist you. Acknowledging past behaviour is also a necessary part of the healing process. It's normal to feel uncomfortable thinking about how badly we've behaved. None of us want to admit to poor behaviour.

In the following exercise, we explore these behaviours. Start by listing the behaviours or actions that have embarrassed or made you feel ashamed. It may have been when you bullied someone or lashed out at a loved one or colleague. It's essential to be honest. Remember, only you see this list. Mine ran to two foolscap pages in length. Take time to reflect on the behaviours you feel bad about and write them all down. Here are some of mine:

- *I have angry reactions, followed by feelings of shame and embarrassment.*

- *I insist on perfection from everyone.*

- *I feel the need to control everything around me.*

- *I threatened a colleague with physical violence.*

- *I find it difficult to show affection or hug someone.*

- *I have difficulty fitting in at social gatherings.*

- *I use sarcasm to deflect compliments as they make me feel uncomfortable.*

- *I sabotage my relationships to avoid getting too close.*

- *I feel lonely, as if I don't belong in this world.*

- *I am focused on sex in my relationships.*

Once you have your list, consider where you can change your behaviour as a first step towards healing. If able to, I recommend apologising to anyone you treated badly. Explain how sorry you are. Make sure you mean it. You can also seek out others who have had experiences similar to yours in forums or men's groups. A shared understanding provides a sense of connection and community. Our self-worth has taken a beating due to our abusive childhood. We need to rebuild our belief and love for ourselves. The following mantra will help in this process. I suggest repeating it at least three times every morning.

 1. *May I be happy and well.*

2. May I be free from pain and suffering.

3. May I have peace in my heart.

Always remember that you are not alone on this journey. Many have experienced similar struggles and are on the same path.

My need to break free from my father's control outweighs my fear of bullying. However, in my urgency to escape, I make an impulsive decision that leads me down a dangerous path. I find myself in need of approval to validate who I am. To get this approval, I do whatever's asked of me. It is the fawn response, a survival tactic. In the next chapter, I'll delve into this response.

Chapter Three

Hiding in Plain Sight

Today is the day. The past months have been miserable, and with a mid-year report card in your pocket, you know what waits. The teacher's comments leave a cold sensation in the pit of your stomach. 'He can do better. He won't concentrate. Plays the fool too much.' Each word hammers home your fate, confirming everything your parents think of you. Shaking your head, *it has to be today.*

Mrs. Leits lives two houses down the street. Each morning, you watch her stagger down the driveway, tattered dressing gown wrapped around her bony frame, arms laden with empty bottles. Smashing glass resonates up and down the street, as she dumps them into her rubbish bin, oblivious to the neighbours' frustration. Then, with a final sweeping look, she shuffles back up the driveway. Your mother complains about the constant flow of people in and out of her house. *It's not right.* But her routine gave you an idea.

Hands trembling, pulling the buff-coloured report card out of your bag. A quick glance to ensure old Watson across the street wasn't watching. She'd come racing over if she saw you, demanding to know what was happening. Lifting the lid of the bin, a swarm of flies erupts. Buzzing angrily, swatting them away, you regather your composure. Taking another quick look up and down the street — no one in sight — quickly shoving the report card under the broken glass and rotting meat scraps, and scurrying home. Every step fearful you were seen. That night, tossing and turning, unable to sleep, ears straining for the sound of the garbage truck. Finally, the squeal of brakes and clatter of bins signal its arrival. With a wave of relief, you drift off to sleep.

***

A week later, you hitchhike a deserted Bagot Road, lowering your thumb, a sigh of frustration. *How much further to this bloody party? Gotta find him if I want the job.*

A Holden Monaro pulls over, shiny chrome mag wheels glinting in the dusk. Black smoke dribbles from its tailpipe. A dark-haired, thin-faced girl pokes her head out and smiles. 'You tired of walking?'

Nodding, rushing toward the car, grateful they stopped.

Her lips stretch into a sneer. 'Then piss in your shoes and swim.' Squeals of laughter erupt inside the car as it surges away, spraying dirt and gravel.

The party is in full swing when you arrive. A girl on hands and knees pukes her guts out in the garden while another holds her hair whispering in her ear. Hesitating, hoping he's still here or the walk in the muggy night, the terrier nipping at your heels, will have been in vain. *He has to be here.*

Stepping over the spread-eagled legs of a boy in the doorway, head lolling to one side, mouth open, a wet patch between his legs. He peers up and mutters, 'Fuck off', then slides sideways, head striking the floor with a *crack*. Smoke hangs above the packed room.

Where is he? A raised arm signals, ignoring it. *I must find him.* Not that you know him well, only by his first name, Trevor. You've seen him at other parties but never spoken to him. Someone told you he needed help where he worked, and you need a job, or it's back to school.

Chants of 'Fight, fight, fight!' come from the rear. Your gut tells you he'll be there. Two girls grapple with each other on the grass, hissing and spitting like wildcats. Clawing at each other's clothes and hair, urged on by the mob. You see him, recognising his hook nose and wine-barrel chest. He looks up, holding your gaze, then turns away. A girl yells triumphantly, waving a tuft of hair above her head. Red lipstick smeared across her face, her T-shirt shredded, exposing a breast. She doesn't care. The defeated girl rolls around on the ground, shrieking and clutching her head. 'Leave my fuckin boyfriend alone', screams the winner and stalks away, a satisfied smile on her face. Laughing in delight, the mob moves inside.

Driven back into the lounge room by the swarming bodies, you search for him.

Out of the mass, an arm wraps around you. Fingers clamp your jaw. A voice rasps, 'I hear you quit school?' His breath is warm on your cheek.

'Um, I, how?'

'I hear stuff. Am I right?' His face inches from yours. Snake eyes flick over you.

Nodding, hoping he understands. The stories about him, *gossip you tell yourself*. 'Uh, I heard you were looking for help?'

'What?'

'I hear you want someone to work for you.' Smirking, white teeth flashing, he nods, releasing your jaw.

'I've never… I know nothing about cars.'

Slapping you on the back, he cackles. 'Don't worry. I'll take care of you.' As he disappears into the crowd, he looks back over his shoulder, mouthing, 'See you Monday'.

***

As you head off for the first day with Trevor, the air hangs like a wet sheet. An hour later, your shirt clings to your back, sweat trickles down your face.

Turning a corner, stepping around a woman seated in front of a laundromat in a plastic fold-up chair, its bottom grazing the pavement. She glances up, then indifferently returns to the magazine on her lap. Lighting a cigarette, taking a long drag, coughs, hawks up a mouthful of phlegm, spitting near your foot. Grimacing, you cross the road to Haan Auto-Electricians.

A pair of legs in blue King Gee shorts and a bent torso over a mudguard are all you can see. *Should I call out?* You cough, no response. Coughing again, louder this time. The blue shorts move. Trevor pokes his head out and stares at you. Recognition slowly dawns on his face, and he ducks back under the hood.

'Shit Haan, it's that kid, the one I told you about.'

A face resembling a dried apple core emerges from the opposite side of the car. Sharp blue eyes scrutinise you.

'Do vat Trevor say.' The apple-core face disappears back under the hood.

'Did you tell your parents you're working here?' Trevor asks, wiping his hands on an oily rag. You recall the conversation.

Your father's finger pointing at your chest, his words spat like venom. 'What?... What? What do you mean? You're not going back to school? Who the hell are you to tell us what you'll do?'

'Umm, there's... I...'

Gathering breath, hands clenched. 'You'll do what I tell you to do. You're not leaving school, and that's final!'

Petulantly, stamping a foot, shouting, 'I can. If I wanna. I got a job, so there.'

His voice hardened as he leaned closer. 'No, you can't sonny. If you don't go to school, you don't live under my roof.' The walls rattle as he slams the front door.

Your mother shakes her head, eyes filled with disappointment.

'Yeah. They think it's great.'

'Good. C'mon, let me show you around. Over there's the boss's office', he says, pointing to a timber-framed glass cubicle. Papers clutter an old wooden desk, two rusted metal chairs stacked in a corner, nothing else in the way of furniture. Above the door, a picture of a woman holding a drill across bare breasts. Her eyes mocking, daring you to look away. 'There's a storeroom out back.' Winking, 'I'll show you that another day.'

'What can I do?'

'What can you do? Good question.' Smiling, punching you on the arm, 'Start by cleaning these.' Nodding at grease-covered tools on the bench, 'I need them done right away. There's a sink near the storeroom. Scrub and rinse 'em, showroom good.' He walks away, whistling.

Three weeks pass, each one blending into the next. The monotony of cleaning tools and greasing bearings grates on your nerves. Desperate for a change, mustering up the courage to approach Trevor. 'Can I work on a car?'

His expression hardens. 'Clean the bloody tools. That's all you're good for.' About to protest, he holds up his right hand, silencing you. 'I'd watch myself if I were you. You can always leave if you don't like it.'

Lowering your eyes, you shut your mouth.

Trevor sniggers. 'If you really want to help, you can with these,' pointing at massive bearings lying on the bench. 'The lubricant and grease are in the storeroom.' It's your first time in the storeroom, which is usually locked.

He motions for you to enter.

Stepping past him, you feel the flat of his hand on your back, shoving you inside.

The door slams behind him. Stumbling, you trip over a can, sending it spinning into a corner and bursting open. Black grease oozes out.

You turn to face him, 'What the...?' The words die in your throat.

Trevor, with legs spread, wields a metal strip that flickers ominously in the harsh fluorescent light. His fingers trace its edge, sending a chill down your spine. 'Jesus, look at the mess you've made,' he muttered, shaking his head with disdain, like a teacher scolding a disobedient child. 'You need to learn a lesson.'

Your heart pounds in your chest as he lets out a cold laugh, the metal strip cutting through the air and biting into your calves.

A cry escapes your lips as you drop to your knees, the pain searing. Trevor silences you with a finger to his lips. 'Shhh, don't let the boss hear.'

Desperately, you scramble across the rough concrete floor, seeking safety in the dimly lit corner. The heavy thud of Trevor's boots echo behind you, accompanied by a menacing snort. 'Where do you think you're going?'

The metal strip tears through your khaki shirt with a sickening rip.

Gasping for breath, tears well in your eyes as he swings again, narrowly missing you and hitting a shelf instead. He drops the strip to the ground with a curse. 'You better learn to keep quiet, or else,' he mutters darkly. 'Now get back outside.'

Shaken, struggling to your feet. As you stare at his retreating back, your heart freezes. You'd wanted him to like you. But the truth dawns. *He's just like my father.*

Reflection: Fawning Behaviour

"Courage starts with showing up and letting ourselves be seen. Because true belonging only happens when we present our authentic, imperfect selves to the world, our sense of belonging can never be greater than our level of self-acceptance. Vulnerability sounds like truth and feels like courage." — Brené Brown

If you've had a traumatic childhood, the only concern we have is survival at all costs. It means we will strive to be good all the time. We sacrifice needs, wants and desires to avoid upsetting anyone, including those who should protect us.

An abused child, instead of reacting to danger by fighting, fleeing or freezing develops a fawning response to hide from conflict or harm. Fawning is a trauma response where we long for acceptance and find that we struggle to assert personal boundaries. We become people-pleasers striving to be likable and become hypervigilant searching for threats. This reaction, of course, will place us in a position where we endure behaviour toward us that others wouldn't tolerate.

We believe we're helping keep the peace when we go into a fawning response. In truth, we're choosing to be invisible and hiding our true feelings. This is because if anyone shows disappointment in us, it would be unbearable. Fawning appears in many ways, which can make it challenging to recognise. Some common fawning responses that you might recognise in yourself are:

- *Always trying to make others happy.*

- *Constantly seeking approval.*

- *Sacrificing your needs to meet others demands.*

- *Going to great lengths to prevent a disagreement or confrontation.*

- *Relying on the opinions of others for your self-worth.*

- *Hiding your true feelings to avoid upsetting others.*

- *Feeling you have to say yes, even when it's not in your best interest.*

- *Holding back your opinions out of fear of criticism.*

- *Taking on difficult responsibilities no one else wants to gain acceptance.*

- *Being alert to others emotions to avoid disappointment.*

- *Striving for perfection to avoid disapproval.*

We often move between these fawning behaviours within our relationships. This further complicates our own understanding of our fawning response.

Adult Reaction: Standing Up

The memory of that storeroom never truly faded. The metal against my skin, the overwhelming fear. Trevor's behaviour was unacceptable, but due to my fawning, I accepted it. My learned behaviour from my father meant it had become what I understood to be the safe choice. Worse than this, I also believed that it was what I deserved. That feeling becomes overwhelming; we see ourselves as simply bad or flawed. Doing anything else would have created greater fear for my inner child and myself.

My behaviour enabled Trevor to see me as an easy target. Abused kids may unwittingly attract their abusers. I don't know what abusers see that others don't, but like an animal sniffing a kill, they seem to be able to hone in on the abused.

My fawning has also caused me to struggle to speak up in meetings, conferences or social gatherings. I desperately want to join the conversation and tell myself I should, but I fear being ridiculed. It's the same if I attend an event or party. I'll hide at the rear, terrified about being called on to speak. If I am, my stomach clenches, I sweat and go red in the face. Fawning will stop us from doing things others take for granted, like returning a meal at a restaurant. Fawning creates a fear of making a fuss. If we do complain, we spend the rest of the night worrying that we'd upset someone and end up wishing we'd never complained in the first place.

All we want is to be part of the group or to be accepted, and we try everything to make this happen. Unfortunately, when we do this, our inner voice can tell us we don't belong or that they don't really like us. To compensate, we're likely to engage in vicious gossip to feel part of the group, even though it might feel shameful as it goes against our authentic selves. It's all about being accepted.

Fawning can also lead us into danger, pulling us into situations that most would question, we ignore. Remember, fawning has been necessary as a survival strategy. In chapter eight, I'll explore the effect of people-pleasing — another way fawning takes hold.

Healing Exercise: Butterfly Hug

Breaking free from the fawn response requires rebuilding self-worth, learning to say no and realising that love and acceptance should never come at the cost of self-sacrifice. Being kind to ourselves is also essential to help the healing process. It takes courage to recognise our fawning responses, but by understanding and being compassionate to ourselves we can begin healing.

Start by listing how you think fawning behaviour has impacted your life. Has it made you uncomfortable or scared? Do you always say yes when asked to help? Even when you have little or no time. Do you avoid speaking out when disagreeing with a conversation, fearing criticism? Reflect on your reactions and consider if you could have responded differently. Once you have your list, please take a moment to study it. Think about the fawning experiences you have engaged in and how you might change those responses. Perhaps, when you have something to say, make sure you speak up. It may feel uncomfortable, but once you do, it will enable you to do so again — until you wonder why you never spoke up in the first place. Or, if you crave approval in a relationship, talk with your partner and make a concerted effort to give rather than take.

The Butterfly hug is an exercise that allows us to touch and hold ourselves lovingly and sympathetically. We engage in self-soothing through touch by combining physical touch with deep breathing. Tapping the meridian points provides a soothing, *relaxing feeling for our inner child and nervous system. I recommend being seated and relaxed before you begin. Take a few deep breaths to settle your heart rate. When ready, start by doing the following:*

1. Cross your hands over your chest.

2. Link your thumbs together to form a butterfly's body.

3. Position your fingertips just below your collarbones.

4. Tap your chest with alternating movements of your hands.

5. Tap with your left hand, then your right hand.

6. Take slow breaths and observe your thoughts and feelings.

7. Continue the exercise for as long as required.

Fawning affects us in numerous ways, which is why I strongly recommend seeking out a professional therapist who specialises in childhood trauma. Seeking help is not a sign of weakness but a step towards healing and self-awareness. These are deep wounds that require careful handling when revisited. I also have resources to assist you and can support your healing journey.

I mistook silence for safety and self-sacrifice for love for a long time. My fawn response stopped me from speaking out about Trevor's behaviour. However, the fawn response didn't let go quickly, and my need to please was intense. It led me into more unhealthy attachments. Next, we will discuss codependency and what it means as adults.

Chapter Four

Illusion of Care

'This yours,' Haan said, in a voice as flat as his desktop. He tapped a rumpled envelope, its edges curling in the oppressive heat. 'Trevor says you not needed.' Pulling a rag from his sweat-soaked overalls, wiping his nose, examining it, shoving it back into his pocket. He tapped the desk again. 'Take it. Find other work.'

'Why? I've done everything…'

Haan cuts you off with a dismissive wave. 'No work. Finish.'

The truth crashes down on you. Trevor had been all smiles this morning, draping a friendly arm around your shoulders, whispering in your ear, 'The boss wants to talk to you.'

Shrugging off his arm, voice trembling. 'Why?'

'He'll be back after two. You'll find out then.' Trevor sauntered away, hands in his pockets, whistling.

Your fingers grip the chair's edge, knuckles whitening with effort. You want to tell him about Trevor, but Haan's gaze slides away — *he knows and doesn't care*. The chair screeches as you stand, grabbing the envelope, leaving without a backward glance. *To hell with him.* Trevor's eyes track every step as you walk out.

Sitting in the grim-looking milk bar, harsh reality sank in. *Should I go home?* Dismissing the thought immediately. *There has to be another way.* Find Larry.

***

Pool Hall is a grand title for a windowless metal shed with dim lighting and smell of stale beer. The man in charge, rumoured to be from Greece, wears a shirt open to his waist, displaying a chest of thick, curly black hair with a chunky gold chain hanging around his neck, catching the light with every movement. You spot Larry leaning against a table.

'Hey, Graham. How's it going?' Larry's voice is warm, but you can't manage more than a shaky smile. The lump in your throat threatens to spill over. Larry places a hand on your shoulder. 'What's up?'

The words spill out. 'They got rid of me at work. Bastards. And I've gotta get out of home.'

Larry's hand falls away, concern in his eyes. 'Geez. That's rough. I'm sure it'll work out.' Your heart sinks as you stare at him. *Is he even listening? It's easy for him to say it'll work out.* Shaking your head, 'Can I stay at your place?'

'Sorry. We got the mob up from Alice. It's nuts at the moment. That's why I'm here. Alex, he might...' Larry gestures towards a man at another table. 'He's got a place near the rail yards. If you got money, bet he'd let you.'

'Ya reckon he might?'

Shrugging, 'Can't hurt to ask. C'mon.'

Alex focused on his shot, muscles taut with concentration. The *crack* of the cue hitting the white ball echoed in the empty pool hall. The white ball zipped across the green baize, slamming into the black with a *clack*, sending it into the corner pocket.

'Great shot.' Larry cheered, clapping his hands with enthusiasm.

Alex acknowledged the compliment with a grunt. 'I've done better.' Larry, face now serious. 'Alex, this is Graham. He needs a place to crash. Can you help him out?'

Alex's gaze sweeps over you, his eyebrows arch in disdain. 'I don't run a squat for every kid in town,' he snorts, leaning on his cue, chalking it with long, deliberate strokes. 'Got any money?'

Your heart leapt. 'Yes, I got paid.' You have the three ten-dollar notes from Haan and a small refund from the hostel — forty dollars in total. 'Some,' you hedge, unwilling to tell him the exact amount.

Alex's expression shifts, calculating. 'Okay. You can crash for a couple of nights. It's nuthin' fancy.' Tossing the chalk onto the table and ramming his cue into the rack. 'I'm heading there now if you wanna come.' He extended his hand. 'Give us some.'

'How, how much do you want?'

Alex's fingers tap restlessly against a pimple on his chin. 'Need smokes and petrol. Reckon twenty should do it... for now.'

His house looked like a storm hammered it. Cardboard slapped against the broken windows, shards of glass crunch beneath your feet on the dirt path. Paint is peeling from the walls in ragged strips, exposing the rotting wood beneath. You shrug with resignation. Beggars can't be choosers. Alex bounded up the steps, kicking open the door and bellowing into the darkness. 'Sam. Get up. You can't sleep all bloody day.' A dishevelled boy on the floor stirs, rubbing his eyes, blinking like a newborn owl. He rises, yawns, and shuffles out of the room, disappearing into the shadows. The door slamming behind him, Alex smirks. 'Welcome to my home. How much did you say you got left?'

Ignoring the question. 'Am I putting him out?'

'Nah. People come and go. Sam's been here a while. I asked how much money you got.'

Pausing, you want to lie, but Alex's expression warns that it might not be the best course of action. If you tell him the truth, he'll take it all. You lie — a bit. 'Um, ten.'

'Good. Need a feed.'

Hamburger aroma drifted through the house and seeped into Sam's dreams. Tottering into the room, hair tousled, shirt undone, tummy bouncing like jelly. Wolfing down his burger, meat, bread and beetroot all disappearing down his throat. With a loud burp, wiping greasy fingers on his shirt, muttering, 'Got any smokes?'

Alex moans. 'Bugger me, Sam.' Flipping a packet of Chesterfields across the table.

Lighting one, Sam blows smoke in your direction. 'Hey, ain't you a friend of Trevor's?'

Your heart freezes.

'Hear he's a bit of a prick.' He sniggered. Turning to Alex. 'There's three of us, we can get the copper.'

Unsure of what he means, and not keen on anything to do with the police, 'What do you mean get the copper? The police? Why?'

Sputtering, Sam says, 'No fuckwit. Copper, wire, copper.' Sneering, he blows more smoke in your direction. 'Shit, where'd you find him, Alex?' Coughing, taking a deep breath, continued, 'Tell him Alex.' Alex, with a humourless grin, 'It's in the rail yard. We're gonna get it.'

'Why?'

Sam rolls his eyes. 'Geez. We sell it, stupid.'

Snorting, Alex glares at Sam. 'Shut up.'

Scratching your head, 'Don't the rail people own it?'

Alex's face darkens. 'No.'

Sam begins to insist. 'C'mon Alex. Let's do it.'

'They're big effen things. It'll take both of youse. You game Graham?' Alex's eyes fix on you.

Sam taunts. 'He's a scaredy cat, aren't you? Scaredy cat, scaredy cat,' poking his tongue out.

Your throat is dry. *What can I do?* Pushing the thought away, you nod.

'I didn't think you'd have the guts. Let's go tonight, Alex. Please,' Sam begs.

'I'm gonna get some sleep. I'll decide later.'

Sam paces up and down, opening cupboard doors, then, in frustration, slamming them shut. Sits, gets up, and then sits again. Alex yells from the bedroom, 'Stop the goddamn noise.'

Sam, irritated, shouts back, 'I'm getting ready.'

'There's nothing to get ready. Shut up or I'll come out and smack you one.'

Crestfallen, Sam slumps beside you.

As dusk settles, Alex reappears, a determined glint in his eye, announcing tonight's the night to get the copper. A chill in your stomach as you get into Alex's car. He slides the Falcon sideways in the dirt, tyres spinning, tearing away from his ramshackle yard. Five minutes later, the headlights slice through the darkness, revealing an overgrown path. The scent of earth in the air as Alex veers onto the dirt track flanked by dense bush. The headlights illuminate disused goods carriages, choked with tangled grass and weeds. The car jolts to a stop in front of a wire fence groaning with each gust of wind. You watch, mesmerised, as it creaks ominously. *How long will it be before it collapses?*

'Climb over here,' Alex says casually.

You look at him, then at the fence, then back at Alex, disbelief etched on your face. Sam remains silent. 'You sure?'

'Yeah,' Alex replies nonchalantly. 'The copper's in front of you once you're over.'

How he knows this, he doesn't explain. The fence continues creaking. You shiver. The thought of climbing the fence and searching the bush in the dark, dodging who-knows-what, fills you with dread. 'How will we find it?'

'They're rolls of copper wire,' Alex snaps. 'There won't be anything else lying on the ground. I'll leave the lights on. Hurry up before someone comes.'

Your mind races with images of snakes, rats, and unseen dangers. Before you can voice your concerns, Alex's temper flares. He lashes out, the back of his hand striking you across the lips. The metallic taste of blood flooding your mouth. 'Go and fuckin' find 'em before I do real damage.' Stung and humiliated, you get out of the car. Sam, trembling, stands beside you, eager to avoid a similar fate. Approaching the fence, the distant hum of engines from the Stuart Highway fills the silence. Sam hesitates, clearly reluctant. You grip the fence, it wobbles dangerously. Glancing back, you see Alex's silhouette, you feel his eyes fixed on you. Placing a foot on the fence, it begins to buckle and sway. Ignoring your instincts, you reach higher for a handhold. The fence groans. At that moment,

Sam decides to join you. With a tortured squeal, the fence collapses under the combined weight. You both sprawl into the rail yard with a jarring crash.

Sam, beside you, moans about his knee. You want to punch him in the head to silence his whimpering. You roll onto your hands and knees and begin crawling forward with deliberate care, testing the ground ahead with your hand. A rustle in the underbrush makes you freeze. Your fingers brush a solid object. You trace its length — thick, rubber coils. *This has to be it.*

Turning back around, Alex is framed by the moon, motionless behind the wheel. The thought of returning empty-handed fills you with dread. Rubbing your bruised lip, you weigh your options. Sam's heavy footsteps crash through the scrub. He drops beside you, panting. 'Shit didn't see you.' Suddenly, everything goes dark. Sam moans, 'He's turned the lights off.'

'You noticed. Got a torch?'

'Did you see me carrying a torch?' He mutters something else that you can't quite make out before giving a low whistle. 'Is this it?' He pats the rubber-covered coil.

'Um, what do you think?' Shaking your head. 'No, don't answer that. What are we gonna do?'

Sam peers up and shouts into the darkness, 'Switch the lights on, Alex.' There's no response, just a deep, enveloping blackness.

'These things are huge, too big to move. Have you or Alex seen them before?'

Sam snaps, 'Don't be stupid. We can't come here during the day. It's private property. Alex said he had.'

With a sinking heart, you suggest, 'Maybe if we drag them?'

Headlights sweep across the yard as another car pulls up. Sam hisses, 'Shit, someone else is here.' Car doors slam, there are raised voices. 'Alex will get rid of 'em.' A torch beam slices through the night, its light darts across the scrub, searching, probing. Sam slides closer, eyes wide with urgency. 'They're coming this way,' he whispers. He's on his feet in a heartbeat, sprinting towards the highway with a speed that leaves you stunned. A greyhound would've had a hard time catching him.

'Hey, you, stop!' a man yelled, tearing after him. Panic grips you. You bolt in the opposite direction, adrenaline surging. At each step, your heartbeat thumps in your ears. Suddenly, the ground vanishes beneath you, plummeting into a concrete drain, the rough surface scrapes your cheek and knees. Huddling in the murky bottom, holding your breath, praying.

Footsteps approach, a gruff voice mutters, 'One ran this way. Don't know what the hell they expect to find.' A muffled voice responds. The torch beam sweeps over the drain, picking out your terrified face. 'C'mon, get out of there, you idiot.' Dragging yourself over the edge, legs trembling, you stand.

'That's him,' Alex declares, stepping into the torchlight.

You gape, surprised. 'He's the one who told us to do it,' pointing at Alex, desperation in your voice. 'He wants to sell it.'

'You piece of shit. I don't know you.'

'That's enough. You can both come with me.' The officer turns to you. 'How old are you, son?'

'Um...'

'C'mon, I don't have all night.'

'Thirteen.'

'Right. I'll contact your parents and get them to meet us at the station.'

No.

Your father's silence speaks volumes during the drive from the police station. The officer let you off with a warning, advising you to stay off private property and choose better friends. Shuffling to your room, you realise you're trapped under your parents' roof until you can find another job.

Reflection: Codependency

"Codependence is being at war with ourselves, which makes it impossible to trust and love ourselves." — Robert Burney

Codependency is a need for approval and recognition. Because our abuse made us feel worthless, we need to feel valued in our relationships. It leads to doing everything we can to hold onto them, even the unhealthy ones. Our need for approval is all-consuming. Due to the neglect and lack of love as a child, we become codependent and have a need to control others to believe we are in control of the relationship. We will constantly check our partners' whereabouts and need to know every detail of their lives. It's about regaining the power we lost as a child.

We all experience codependency differently depending on the extent and type of trauma we suffered. These are the ways in which our codependency is likely to surface:

- *Neediness — craving attention and reassurance.*

- *Low self-esteem — seeing ourselves as flawed and unworthy of love and respect.*

- *People-pleasing — believing that love is something that we need to earn.*

- *Communication — finding difficulty in communicating effectively.*

- *Poor boundaries — not knowing what healthy boundaries look like.*

- *Difficulty trusting — believing we can't trust or rely on others.*

- *Shame — a feeling that we don't deserve happiness.*

- *Guilt — feeling responsible for people or things out of our control.*

- *Reactivity — having emotional outbursts and overreactions to criticism.*

- *Control — feelings of helplessness and lack of power contribute to controlling behaviours.*

For those of us who have codependency, we'll struggle to have healthy, loving relationships.

Adult Reaction: Risky Behaviour

I should've understood Alex's behaviour as a clear danger sign. But to me, his demands, temper and unpredictability felt familiar, an environment I knew and one in which I could survive. I met him again after the incident with the copper wire. This time, he planned to steal wheel trims from a car yard. I agreed to go along, but I was scared to participate. I stayed in his car while he and another boy snuck into the car yard. The yard was directly across the road from an all-night taxi service, where a woman noted our number plate. The police revisited my home. By then, I'd left.

Rather than walking away, my reaction was to follow and do as he said. My need for a relationship with him, even an abusive one, overrode all else. With codependency, we surrender our wants and desires to avoid conflict, staying silent to maintain peace. If someone is interested in us, we become hooked and remain. Sadly, it's reflective of domestic violence, where the victim will return to the relationship time after time because they are codependent.

I didn't understand my behaviour in my early relationships; even when I did, acting appropriately and being authentic was challenging. As an adult with poor relationship skills, I often became overly clingy or emotionally over-connected by trying to predict my partner's emotional needs. I struggled to make decisions relating to the relationship or would get angry when the other person made a decision. Codependency makes us want constant reassurance and approval. If invited to a party or event, I would hesitate and act as if I didn't want to go. I needed to be asked several times before agreeing to ease my neediness. I had a loving relationship after my divorce, which filled me with joy. I felt valued and noticed. However, when the relationship ended, I remember how distraught I was, to the extent of lying on the lounge room floor, physically feeling my heart tearing in two. Over time, codependency leads to emotional exhaustion and a lack of true intimacy. Because we fear abandonment, we can't give our true selves to the relationship. Paradoxically, this will guarantee the end of our relationship unless we understand and make an effort to change.

Healing Exercise: Being Still

Healing from codependency requires deep self-awareness and boundary-setting. It begins with recognising the unhealthy patterns of self-sacrificing, people-pleasing and the need for external validation. Building a strong sense of yourself is crucial. To do this, reconnect with your needs and determine appropriate boundaries without feeling guilty. It will ensure we break the cycle of doing everything for others.

Self-care means different things to different people. For some, it may be a meditation retreat. For others, it's spending time in nature or time with friends. Determine your own self-care needs. Listen to your body and feel how it reacts to what you do. The best way to do this is through your intuition, not logic. Think about what might make you happy or relaxed. It might be pole dancing, cycling or training for a marathon. Your body and your intuition will tell you what is right. If it feels right, then do it. Whatever you choose to do, continue to undertake it regularly, as this assists in the healing process.

Love is also essential — love for ourselves and someone else. Love softens us and helps us talk about our trauma. At first, it may not be easy to accept love, but if we have a partner with whom we can share our story and willing to provide support, we can begin to let go of codependency. Another way to heal is through play. As abused children, we had less play in childhood than we should've. Our sole focus was on survival. As adults, we should rediscover the joy of playing a game of cards with friends, puzzles, crafts such as pottery or painting, music, singing or dancing. Any of these will help bring joy to our wounded inner child.

Because our nervous system has remained on heightened alert for so long, it can be difficult to find calm. Our busy environment can stimulate and trigger childhood traumas every day, so it's essential to find time to calm our senses. In this next exercise, I invite you to embrace stillness and calm for your inner self. Find a quiet space where you can sit or lie down.

1. *Relax your body.*

2. *Close your eyes and take a few deep breaths.*

3. *With each breath, invite a sense of stillness into your body and mind.*

4. *Let go of the need to do, achieve, or think.*

5. *Be present in the quiet of the moment.*

6. *Each time you breathe, experience the depth of stillness coming over you.*

When ready, write down how you felt. Our authentic self is valuable and the essence of who we are. We may not feel it right now, but it is. Always consider professional help if you require it. Our childhood traumas are deep and complex; professional help will guide us in resolving them.

Codependency is just one of the many wounds carried by my inner child. Beneath the compulsive need to please, to avoid conflict, and to keep others happy lies something more — shame. A belief that I am unlovable, no matter how much I give. It drives my decision to seek approval in an unexpected encounter. It is a turning point, a defining event that shapes my life. How do we overcome shame? Let's find out in the next chapter.

Chapter Five

Whispers in the Dark

Chest pumped, striding towards the Vic Hotel, you're eager to meet your friends. The thirty dollars is burning a hole in your pocket.

It's Friday, and the Vic is buzzing. Sneaking in through the beer garden, you weave through office workers mingling with labourers fresh off building sites, relieved to escape the sweltering sun. Hippies frequent the pub, too. It's close to the Esplanade where they camp. In the centre of a grassed patch, a girl in a flowing skirt and midriff top twirls and jumps. She waves her arms above her head, exposing unshaven armpits. A feather band wrapped around her head. She dances to a tune only she can hear, oblivious to the crowd. The locals call them bludgers, though never to their faces, but you envy their carefree spirit, their loud, unapologetic laughter. Yet, you mimic the locals, wary of becoming a target of their scorn.

At the rear of the beer garden, Roger sits with his brother Greg. A year ahead of you in school, Roger is big; he plays front-row forward for a local League team. Greg works on prawn trawlers plying in and out of Darwin Harbour, his need for a shower increasingly evident the closer you get. Two strangers — a girl with her arm around the shoulders of an older man sit with them. Their heads are close together, glancing up as you approach. The man's face bears a white slash from cheekbone to lip, his clothes patched and stained.

You sit next to the girl, who looks at you with her large puppy eyes. Running her tongue over cracked lips she extends a hand. 'Hiya. I'm Suzy,' she said, a flicker of interest in her eyes.

Smiling, taking the offered hand. The man leant across, wrenching her hand back. 'Behave, bitch.' With a yelp, she lowers her head, tucking her hand under her arm. Greg ignores the altercation, intent on his beer. Roger's already left without saying a word.

'Wanna beer?' Greg asks, placing an empty on the table among a litter of others. 'Hope you've got money. We're out.'

'A little.'

Giggling, Suzy says, 'Great.'

Leaning across the table, Greg holds out his hand. 'I'll get you one and one for me.' He laughs as he heads to the bar, other patrons giving him a wide berth.

An hour drags by. Roger has still not returned. Greg slumps in his chair, head on his chest, snoring softly. Glancing at Suzy, wanting to start a conversation, but she turns away, back to the older man, whispering, snickering, patting his cheek, muttering under her breath. She sneaks a glance at you, then nods, a sly smile on her lips. She suddenly erupts into a coughing fit, her chair rocks backward. You reach out, to steady it. She smiles, displaying uneven and discoloured teeth, whispering, 'Thanks.' Leaning forward, her arm brushes against yours. A fire smoulders in your stomach. 'Got a girlfriend?' her voice teases. Blushing, looking away. The man's eyes move between you and her, filled with suspicion. Suzy giggles, 'Would ya like one?' She's overcome by another coughing fit, spitting on the grass between her feet. 'That's betta. Well, do ya?' The man's eyes are cold as ice. Suzy doesn't seem to notice or care. Reaching across the table, she grabs the cigarette pack, shaking it in frustration. 'Shit, it's empty. I need a smoke. I got sum in my room.' She winks, nudging you. Your heart races.

Slamming his fist on the table the man stands and storms off, elbowing out of the way those too slow to get out of his way. Suzy places a hand on your leg, squeezing. Jerking back, startled, glancing around nervously to see if he's coming back, as her expression saddens. 'Aww. Don't you like me?'

Heart pounding, caught between fear and fascination. 'I, um, I um...'

'C'mon, let's get me smokes.' Her hand slips into yours. A mix of warmth and urgency bubbles inside you as she leads the way to the back of the hotel and up the stairs. At the top, pausing, looking at you. 'You alright?' Your throat constricts. You nod. 'Good, I hope this is working,' she says, grabbing between your legs, sending a surge of pleasure through you.

Hot air erupts from the room as she opens the door. A ceiling fan struggles to move the thick, clammy heat. Whirling around to face you, a mischievous glint in her eyes, tongue between her teeth. She slips the straps of her dress off her shoulders, letting it cascade to the floor. Faded bruises pattern her stomach, each the size of a fist. Her breasts resemble fried eggs, lying flat on her chest. Your eyes glance down to the fuzz below her stomach. Giggling at the expression on your face, she places a hand over her breasts and steps towards the bed, slipping under the sheet. Stretching her arms above her head, motioning for you to join her. 'Get 'em off. I'm waiting.'

Ripping your T-shirt over your head, tossing it aside, you fumble with your belt buckle. It refuses to budge. She watches in silence, her eyes shining with unspoken thoughts. Finally, the buckle clicks open and your jeans slide down to your ankles, kicking them across the room, hustling to the bed, you join her under the sheet. Suzy smiles, wrapping her fingers around your cock. Her grip tightens, your back arches in pleasure.

Laughing, she teases, 'Oh, you like that, do you? Well, I like this.' She places a hand on top of your head and murmurs, 'Do it,' pushing your face down between her open legs. Her voice drops to a hoarse whisper, 'Kiss me there.'

Unsure of what to do, you bury your face between her legs. The sharp scent of sour sweat and stale piss makes your stomach churn. Sliding back up, stammering, 'I... I can't. I don't.'

With an exasperated sigh, she snaps, 'Fuck it. I'm going to get a beer.' Grabbing a packet of Peter Stuyvesant off the bedside, dressing, she leaves you in a whirl of confusion and longing. Punching the pillow, furious with yourself. A creaking floorboard brings a glimmer of hope that she's returned. Turning towards the door, smiling, ready to apologise and a promise to try whatever she wants. The man with the scar leans against the door jamb. Bloodshot eyes sweep around the room before settling on you. Stepping inside, he closes the door. The key turns with a *clunk*. His boots thud on the timber floor. A vein in his forehead pulses. He grips the metal bed frame, muscles rippling up and down his forearms. Fear washes over you.

'I, uh, she, she's gone.'

'I sees you watching me.' His eyes continue to dart around the room, as if he expects her to reappear, then fix back on you.

Your jeans are on the other side of the room, where you'd kicked them in your haste to get to her. He's between them and you. 'I... I... is she...?'

'She's filth, that's what she is.'

Slipping out of the bed, wrapping the rumpled sheet around your waist, avoiding looking into his eyes. 'I didn't...'

With the speed of a striking snake, his fingers close around your throat, crushing your windpipe as he pushes you against the wall. White spots dance before your eyes, your vision blurring as you fight for breath. 'I don't want that bitch,' he growls, his grip tightening. With a harsh tug of your hair, he forces your head back against the wall, his face inches from yours. His eyes, pitiless and cold, bore into you. A steel blade presses against your cheek. You want to resist, but a voice inside whispers you're getting what you deserve.

'I'll cut you from fuckin ear-to-ear if you make a sound. You want this.' he sneers.

'No... please, no.'

Spinning you around, he shoves you face-first onto the mattress, its musty smell haunting you of her. 'You do. I know,' he taunts.

The blade rests against your throat. His belt hits the floor with a thud.

Your fingers claw at the sheet to escape his grasp. With a snicker, he grabs your ankles, pulling you back and twisting your arm behind you. His breath is hot against your ear. He grunts, 'Take it in your hand.'

Then, with a howl, he thrusts himself on you. Tears stream down your face as you feel him, his roughness. Lying motionless, allowing him to do as he pleases.

Later, amidst bloodstained sheets, shuddering at the memory of his presence. You know he saw you as an object to be used and discarded. Spinning around, you half-expect to see him leering at you — a sigh of relief. The room is empty.

Muffled laughter drifts up from the hotel below. A certainty grips you — no one can know. If anyone found out, you'd be a joke for years.

It is a secret you vow to keep, whispering to yourself that it never happened. One day, perhaps, you'd believe it. Gritting your teeth, you dress. With trembling steps, leave the room.

Reflection: Toxic Shame

"We live in a world where most people still subscribe to the belief that shame is a good tool for keeping people in line. Not only is this wrong, but it's dangerous. Shame is highly correlated with addiction, violence, aggression, depression, eating disorders, and bullying." — Brené Brown

We all experience shame at some point in our lives. Healthy shame is good. It helps us understand when we do something wrong and have regrets. For example, I'm ashamed of leaving my three children when my marriage failed. I understand and recognise it, but it doesn't determine my every emotion. This shame can pass.

Toxic shame, on the other hand, does not pass. As children, when trapped in a repetitive abusive environment the shame becomes toxic. Like all childhood abuse it develops from a family environment devoid of love and care and has long-lasting effects. It's at the core of our sadness, loneliness, anger, rage and feeling that there is something wrong with who we are. The feeling for many is that we are not wanted and don't belong here.

Toxic shame is so locked into our physical and emotional body that when we want or desire something we feel self-loathing or self-contempt for ourselves as if we don't deserve anything good or nice. We have thoughts such as 'I'm not good enough,' 'No one cares about me,' or 'I can't achieve anything because I don't deserve it.' These are difficult to dismiss as they've been with us since childhood.

We face addiction to alcohol, drugs, food, pornography and sex. These are used to numb our childhood trauma. Toxic shame also has a physical impact on us such as increased sweating, lump in the throat, clenched stomach or throwing up. Without healing, our toxic shame will continue to drive our insecurities, fears, and feelings of unworthiness.

Adult Reaction: Deserving Better

How did I get into that situation in the hotel room? I don't know. I suspect my addiction to sex. My teenage brain wanted sex and attention at any cost.

Toxic shame creates such a strong belief that we are unworthy that I believed the only love I deserved was in the form of abuse. This may not be easy to comprehend; rape is rape. But survivors of rape react differently depending on their circumstance. I cannot convince myself that I didn't deserve what happened. No matter how hard I try. My feelings of shame didn't begin with the rape, that happened years before, but the rape reinforced the toxic shame. As with Trevor and his mistreatment in the storeroom, I didn't question this either. I accepted it. My core belief was that I was unworthy and what happens to me is my fault. We keep quiet about our abuse and the thoughts it generates, terrified of what might happen if others find out. These fears keep toxic shame secretive. This continues into adulthood. We have all heard of someone who has appeared to have it all to live for suddenly taking their own life. None of us knows what another person is struggling with. I can tell you from my own experience that even in my darkest moments I've smiled and appeared happy to my friends. We struggle to talk about our trauma because we fear judgment or rejection.

Abused children see things in black and white. If we're not loved, then we're unlovable by all and there must be something wrong with us. Our reasoning is different to those who haven't been abused. We lose perception of right and wrong, good or bad.

For me, my shame appears in many ways, sometimes violent but often in a way that highlights my low self-esteem. For example, when I go to walk in or out of a doorway and someone else is walking towards me, I step aside and mumble an apology when there is nothing to apologise for. It's an automatic reaction to feeling that I am less than them. My shame also lives in my head. It tells me I can't do something or I won't succeed no matter what I do. The same happens if I want to talk to someone new. My toxic shame surfaces and tells me I'm not interesting and they won't want to talk to me. Have you felt similar emotions? Toxic shame can be triggered far more easily as we get older, which is why we need to heal no matter our age.

Healing Exercise: Emotional Recovery

First we need to recognise that we are not responsible for our abuse. Healing begins when we understand that toxic shame is not ours to carry. To begin, explore the good things about yourself to find your own self-worth. Write down everything that is good about you. Study what you've written and remember that your life has been productive and worthwhile, even though you carry toxic shame. To rebuild self-worth, we need empathy and love for ourselves and others. The more we do this, the more we heal.

We also need to change our emotional responses. Whenever you feel anxious, take a deep breath and think about what's happening. Is your heart racing? Are you feeling sick in the stomach? Then ask, why am I getting so upset? What can I do differently? Challenging our emotional reactions or negative thoughts allows us to change our perspective. A simple method when you feel anxious is to place a hand on your chest, take a deep breath and tell yourself it's alright. Keep saying this until your nervous system calms down.

It's important to be gentle with ourselves and to feel our feelings. Don't deny them and don't rush them; let them flow naturally. Changing toxic shame will not happen overnight. It takes time. Toxic shame is complex and may require a therapist skilled in working with shame-based trauma to assist you. Some of the therapies to consider include:

- *Cognitive Behavioural Therapy — talk therapy that helps you manage your trauma by changing the way you think and behave.*

- *Compassion-focused Therapy — helps you acquire the skills to develop the key attributes of compassion, distress tolerance, empathy and non-judgment.*

- *Emotional Freedom Technique — involves tapping your fingertips on specific points on your hands, face and body while focusing on your thoughts and feelings.*

- *Eye Movement Desensitisation and Reprocessing — recalling traumatic memories while following a therapist's eye movement instructions.*

- *Hakomi Therapy — guides the client without imposing perceptions or preferences, adjusting to the client's needs.*

- *Hypnotherapy — uses hypnosis to gain control over traumatic events and behaviours that need to change.*

- *Psychology — removes toxic shame by identifying the root causes of shame, cultivating self-compassion and healthy coping mechanisms.*

- *Quantum Healing Hypnosis Technique — healing through the experiences of our Past Lives.*

- *Somatic Therapy — explores how the body expresses painful experiences, applying mind-body healing to aid trauma recovery.*

Healing is about unlearning the toxic shame. I'm here to offer you support and guidance on that healing path. The following will help manage your nervous system and I recommend that you undertake it daily as repetition is important in healing. This practice is known as Grounding Breath or Box Breathing. The breathing is done through your nose with your mouth closed.

1. *Close your eyes.*

2. *Breathe in on a four count.*

3. *Hold for a four count.*

4. *Breathe out on a four count.*

5. *Hold for a four count.*

6. *Breathe in on a four count.*

7. *Hold for a four count.*

8. *Breathe out on a four count.*

Feel how quickly you become more grounded and calmer. To understand more about how toxic shame impacts us read Healing The Shame That Binds You *by John Bradshaw.*

After the rape, I found myself engaging in a self-destructive and reckless cycle in an attempt to numb the shame. But the shame was passed down from generation after generation. My father had his demons. His anger and fury were beyond his control. In the next chapter, I'll explain how intergenerational trauma decides our fate long before we're born and answer whether we can free ourselves from this trauma.

Chapter Six

Edge of Collapse

The wind whipped sand across Fannie Bay beach, stinging your cheeks as you emerged from the sailing club, thoughts thickened by alcohol, every step uncertain. A boy and a girl huddle near the club, sipping from a Fanta bottle. Who are they fooling? A year ago, you'd done the same.

Suddenly, a rumble cut through your thoughts — a familiar voice called your name from behind the glare of approaching headlights. Squinting, you recognise Ethan from the workshop, where he scavenged car parts from Trevor.

'Hey, mate. How the hell are you?' His words slurred as he leaned out of the window. You rest against the rumbling bonnet. 'Grea... great car.'

'Yeah, it goes like a rocket.' Beside him sat Larry's brother Alan, expression blank. The scent of beer wafts from the open window — empty bottles scattered in the backseat.

'C'mon, hop in. I'll take you for a spin.' You hesitate, he's pissed. But a voice whispers, *why not? No one gives a shit about you anyway.* You climb into the backseat behind Ethan. He revs the engine and spins the wheels, sending stones and sand flying as the car fishtails onto the road.

Gripping the seat, you begin to regret your decision. With a deep breath, curling your legs up, praying for it to end soon. Alan turned, offering a beer.

You couldn't refuse — not in Darwin. Turning back, he stuck his head out the window, yelling, 'Bloody awesome, yeah.'

Peering over Ethan's shoulder, the speedometer needle is at the top of the glowing dial. Houses blur past. Darwin High disappears in a flash. Ethan heads towards Mindil Beach. Eyes shut, hoping he'll slow down, the engine's roar changes.

'Fuck! They're going too slow.'

Your eyes snap open to see three small faces staring back from a station wagon, too close for comfort. Ethan screams, 'We're gonna hit 'em.' Swerving the car into oncoming traffic, a truck horn blares, its lights blinding.

Slipping between the truck and the station wagon, the Valiant spins wildly — the smell of burning rubber in the air. A metallic taste fills your mouth. Later that night, the doctor tells you it was fear.

Time freezes, every detail etched in your mind — the twisting car, Alan wrapping his arms around his chest, the looming Coconut tree, the sickening impact.

BANG! CRUNCH!

Metal screeches and glass shatters. Alan's head strikes the tree. He slumps like a deflated balloon. Ethan sprawls across the steering wheel; you're thrown upwards, striking the roof and then hurled back into your seat. Knee trapped between the front and back seat. Dazed, stars shine above. Where's the roof?

Rushed to the emergency, bloodied, stretcher wheels squeaking. The harsh lights, disinfectant and chaos erase the dance from your memory.

Sitting on a hard plastic chair in the emergency room, bandages wrapped around your head and knee, eyelids drooping as you fight an overwhelming urge to sleep.

You have to figure out how to get home. The police had been bombarding you with questions. Dissatisfaction with your answers was evident as they pressed whether any of you'd been drinking. You remained silent.

The room is empty, except for a boy sitting at the far end. You think you recognise him, but it hurts to concentrate.

He stands and walks toward you. Anxiety tightens your chest, watching him approach. He's older, stout and solid, no trace of fat, but he appears burdened as if carrying the world on his shoulders. He drops into the seat next to yours.

You struggle to remember his name. *Paul? Roger? No. Danny. Yes, Danny. That's it.*

Out of the corner of your eye, you see him studying your bandaged knee and head.

'You okay?'

Not sure what he wants, you nod, immediately regretting it as pain shoots through your skull. 'Umm, yeah. Were you at the dance?'

A quick shake of his head. 'No. I work here, in the hospital. I heard some young people were in an accident.'

You bristle at the reference, watching his face for a hint of condescension, but decide he doesn't mean it as an insult. Head buzzing from whatever the nurse gave you, you struggle to focus. 'Are you a... a friend of...?'

He interrupted, 'I know Alan.'

A wave of realisation washes over you. 'Alan... how is he?'

His face tightens, looking away, the weight on his shoulders seems even heavier. 'He's in surgery. It's bad.'

The room feels colder, the sound of the hospital fades into a dull hum. You want to say something, but the words stick in your throat. Instead, you both sit silently.

He breaks the silence. 'Oh, I'm Danny by the way.'

'Yeah. Hi. I'm, uh, I'm Graham.' Fighting the throbbing in your head, you tell him what happened. 'Alan. His, his head, he, it hit, hit the tree. It was terrible. He just...' Your voice trails away. The picture of Alan's head bouncing off the tree trunk sends a shiver through your body. *What else can I say?*

Danny exhaled. 'Yeah, and the bloody driver only got a bruised rib. Can you believe it?'

'He was flying.'

'When will your parents get here?'

'Uh, no, they're not.'

'Use the phone here to call them. The nurses will let you.'

Turning away, hiding the fear in your eyes, 'Really, it's okay. I don't wanna. They... they wouldn't understand.'

'It was an accident, of course, they will.'

'I'll find my way home.'

'I've finished work and can give you a lift. If you want, that is?' Your stomach clenches at the thought of getting back in a car. 'Did the doctor say you could go?'

'Yeah. He said it'd be okay.' It's what else he said that haunted you. 'If you'd hit the roof a little higher, it would have taken your head off.'

Tiptoeing to your bedroom, dropping into bed, exhausted, knowing the morning will bring trouble. You can hear them now. *What have you been up to? Why do you keep doing these stupid things?* Drifting into a fitful sleep, haunted by visions of tiny, terrified faces and Alan's head splitting open on a coconut tree.

***

The morning brings a level of pain you haven't felt before. Blood seeps through the bandage around your head. A glance in the mirror shows a red dot surrounded by white. Each movement sends a shooting pain through your knee and increases the throbbing in your head. The thick dressing makes it difficult to move at anything faster than a hobble. Your shirt, stiff with dried blood. *No point changing. I've gotta get out of here.*

Ear pressed against the door, straining to hear any movement in the house. Opening the door, peeking up and down the hallway, inching out of the bedroom, grasping a glass louvre for balance. A shudder runs through you, remembering Alan. *I hope he's okay.*

Taking a deep breath and readying yourself, studying the length of the hallway. *Can I make it? I have to before they see me.* The first step sends your knee screaming in protest. You lean against the louvre windows, waiting for it to ease. The bandage around your head loosens, a drop of blood falls to the floor. *Bet they make me clean that up.*

Voices echo from the kitchen. Taking another step, wobbling, grabbing hold of another louvre. Drowning in fear, you take one more step.

Your mother walks around the corner and stops, her hand flies to her mouth as she lets out a blood-curdling scream. 'What? What have you done? Laurie! Laurie! Come and see this.'

Chair legs scrape on the floor. Your father storms around the corner, annoyed at having his breakfast interrupted. He halts, mouth open. 'What...?' His voice trails off as he takes in your messy, blood-soaked state.

Stammering, 'I... I...' The night's events crash down, your knees buckle. You hold on to the louvre, desperate not to fall to the floor.

Your mother continues screeching like a demented cockatoo. 'It's those friends of his. They're trouble. He doesn't listen.' The vitriol in her voice shakes you to the core.

Stalking towards you, eyes blazing, your father glares. He stands five foot five in his socks — solid, broad-shouldered, a former army middleweight boxing champion — and that's who he's become. Jaw jutting out, hands clenched, contempt drips from his voice. 'What have you been up to now?'

Back-pedalling, there's a crack, like a rifle shot in the narrow hallway, as a louvre snaps in two, a sliver of glass piercing your shoulder. Raising your hands to protect yourself, Old Spice overpowering as he moves closer.

'Don't raise your hands to me, sonny. I've beaten better men than you.' Fists cocked, he waits... Instead of hitting you, an expression of disgust crosses his face.

His anger and rejection fuelled the years of pent-up hate. You can see in his eyes his inability to stop.

Your anger pours out. You scream, no longer caring what he might do. 'My friend's in hospital and might die, and you don't care about anything but yourself.' With a sob, 'Fuck you.'

Leaning in, his eyes devoid of sympathy. 'GET OUT OF MY HOUSE!' Turning his back, he walks away.

A stabbing pain sears your chest. You understand it's over.

Each step brings a fresh wave of pain as you make your way out of the house. Your father's words echo in your ears. *Too fuckin' right, I will.* Passers-by avert their eyes or find something interesting on the opposite side of the street. Heading to the bus shelter at Parap shops, *it'll be quiet on a Sunday morning,* and you can't think of anywhere else to go. Collapsing onto the bench, ignoring the ripe stench of piss and vomit. Resting your back against the wall, longing for a family life that is normal and loving. You exhale, as tears begin to roll down your cheeks.

A horn blast jolts you back to reality, shielding your eyes from the sun, you see Danny leaning out of his car window, motioning for you to come over.

The pounding in your head intensifies as you struggle to stand, limping towards him.

Concern is etched on his face. 'What are you doing there?'

How do I explain? 'Argument... at home.'

He nods sympathetically, though you're not sure he truly understands. But the effort is appreciated. 'What will you do?'

Letting out a heavy sigh, shoulders slumping. 'Find somewhere else to live.'

'My old man's got a caravan. It's out of town, but you can stay there. And I can ask at work if they need anyone.'

A smile breaks across your face, the first in what feels like forever.

Not wanting a repeat of that morning's argument, you sneak into your bedroom late at night, quietly gathering your clothes, wondering if anyone will even notice you're gone. With a heavy heart, you accept that they probably won't. Two weeks later, you're working alongside Danny in the Darwin Hospital laundry.

Reflection: Intergenerational Trauma

"By the turning of this wheel, karmic suffering repeats, and trauma is transmitted from one generation to the next — until it finds space and presence and clarity; until it is owned so that it may be healed." — Thomas Hübl

Intergenerational trauma is about the passing of unresolved trauma from one generation to the next. If our caregivers grew up in a violent household, they might believe that abuse is a form of love and is normal behaviour. Their lack of awareness continues through generations. In fact, scientific study suggests that generational trauma can lead to future generations being more susceptible to stress, anxiety and depression. The study suggests that children can inherit stress responses even when they didn't experience an original trauma. To avoid passing on trauma, it's important to understand our caregivers' background and the trauma associated with their upbringing. We need to find ways to break the intergenerational trauma cycle.

Adult Reaction: Parent Trauma

My father's childhood trauma drove him to be the violent man he was. Whenever he felt shamed by me, his reaction was physical. It's all he knew because of his childhood experiences. His actions when I stood in front of him, wrapped in bandages, highlighted how deep his generational trauma was. He didn't ask what happened. Or, was I alright? No, his reaction was to inflict more pain and hurt. His only known way to respond was with violence and his fists. My father never understood or healed his trauma, and he didn't know it drove him to these acts of violence. He just mirrored what he learnt as a child.

I don't think my father saw me as a child. When I was five, he took me to a farm and into a shed with a pit in its centre. In the pit were two fighting Cocks. It was brutal watching these birds tear each other apart. The men around the pit were placing bets, laughing and yelling at the birds. My father participated in both. I trembled watching those birds, as it wasn't long after the incident in the forest. My heart raced at what I was witnessing. I felt frightened and alone among these grown men. No one took any interest in me. I don't know why he took me. Did he forget I was with him? Was I an inconvenience that didn't matter? Perhaps his own needs and desires overcame his concern for my well-being. I remember a smile of satisfaction on his face as we left. I can't explain his reasoning other than that he may have had narcissistic tendencies, and no one mattered but him. Another result of the abuse he suffered as a child.

I know my father's background. My sister researched our family history and discovered a sister he didn't know living in Wales. The sister explained how violent and abusive their father was. She also said my father was given to a couple in England after his mother died in childbirth. I imagine he was terrified to be treated like that at such a traumatic time, losing his mother. Given away like a disposable item. How would he have self-worth after that? My father didn't know the effects of his childhood abuse. That's no excuse for the treatment he metered out. But it is an explanation and helps me understand intergenerational trauma. It's also an insight into how difficult it is to break the cycle of intergenerational trauma. I remember the last time I saw him alive. He was lying in a nursing home bed, incapacitated by a stroke. He wanted me to shave his face as he hadn't been shaved in days. I didn't want to be near him. But I couldn't refuse. I felt uncomfortable touching him even in the slightest way. At the end of the shave, I made my exit. It was the last time I saw him alive. I have remorse and guilt about how I felt, but I know that any connection with him ended many years earlier. However, I found a way to forgive. Let's explore how.

Healing Exercise: Revisiting the Past

Acknowledging that we have intergenerational trauma is the first step in healing. This may bring up painful memories of family history, but it's important to understand and know where the trauma began. You may find it goes back several generations.

Our healing involves creating a positive new story about ourselves. We must break negative beliefs through the use of affirmations to build positive beliefs about ourselves. Affirmations such as 'I am capable' or 'I will practice daily to improve myself.' These build and change the perception we have of ourselves.

Forgiveness plays a crucial role in healing from childhood trauma. If we don't forgive, we will remain stuck in the past, reliving our traumas. It took me a long time to forgive my father. However, once I understood that my poor behaviour as an adult was related to my childhood abuse, I understood that my father's behaviour was also related to his abuse. He could no more control his reactions than he could hold back a raging river. Once I came to this realisation, I began to release my anger. A sense of relief and freedom followed. We hear that forgiving is the only way to move on with our lives. I now know this to be true.

To start the process of forgiving, undertake the following exercise as developed by John Bradshaw. We will revisit our family and feel the events that happened to us. It's important that you guide and support your inner child through this exercise. You can do this by connecting with it as you begin and letting it know it's safe and that you will be here to comfort it every step of the way.

This exercise may bring up other traumas. If it does, stop and seek professional help.

To begin, answer the questions from the perspective of your inner child. Then, consider answering as your caregiver would. Finally, answer them from your point of view as an adult today.

1. *Start by closing our eyes and taking a few deep breaths.*

2. *When ready, go back to your childhood home.*

3. *Look in the window and see yourself inside.*

4. *Take a moment and consider what you see.*

5. *Take a moment and consider how you feel.*

When finished, journal your responses with the following questions?

- *What did the memories bring up?*

- *What beliefs have been passed from one generation to another?*

- *What did you feel and see?*

- *What shaped your caregivers?*

- *Was it anger or hurt?*

- *How were you treated?*

- *Did this impact their caregiving?*

Write down everything that comes to mind. Healing is a process. To forgive, we need to feel the pain and process it to break our intergenerational trauma. Our caregivers didn't, as they weren't aware of the effect of their childhood abuse. By acknowledging our past and understanding what happened to us means we can rewrite our present and create a healthier future. Forgiving requires patience, self-reflection, and understanding. When we realise that they had an abusive childhood, it's easier to understand their trauma and the responses they had as adults. Once we do this, we can find forgiveness.

If our fathers never received love, how could they possibly show love? And yet, a father's love is essential to our sense of self-worth and emotional well-being. When love is absent, we develop wounds that follow us into adulthood. In the next chapter, we'll explore the father wound and uncover how the lack of that love influences our relationships today.

Chapter Seven

Road to Nowhere

Danny grabbed your arm. 'Hey. Did you hear what I said?'

'Huh, what?'

'Your friend, Pig. You reckon he might have some grass?'

'It's Pug, and he's not my friend.' Pug is Adrian, but never call him that if you value your health. Pug has hands that can crush a beer can in seconds. His face looks like it might have been a punching bag in his early years. Messing with Pug was not smart. But in Darwin, if you want grass, the drive-in is the place to go, and Pug is the person to see.

You met him at school when the teachers, in their infinite wisdom, decided to dump you in the difficult boys' class. Pug was there; he didn't last long. He was expelled for decking a teacher. You'd always sought out the strongest person you could without knowing why, even if they were dangerous, as Pug was. He commanded respect in a way that you never did. Evans was still a problem. But you'd managed to avoid a second beating. Unlikely you could escape him forever. You'd heard he was looking for you. Having Pug around provided you with a feeling you rarely felt. Safety. Pug's friendship ensured that the bullying stopped — nobody dared mess with you when you knew Pug.

His pride and joy was a 1966 Holden HR, always parked in the same spot: two rows from the snack bar and the tenth car along.

He greeted you with his usual, 'How are you, Pommy?' Another nickname that stuck from school, much to your dismay. You brace yourself, knowing the crushing grip that's coming. Wincing, you shake his hand.

'I'm good.'

He nods without a smile. 'I hear Alan's fucked up.'

'Yeah.' You want this to be over quickly. Pug can go from friendly to attack without raising a sweat. 'Have you got any stuff, uh, grass?'

He's silent momentarily, his eyes darting behind him and to either side. The hairs on your neck prickle, an uneasy feeling settling in your stomach.

'How much do you want?'

You swallow. 'I don't have much money,' nervously glancing around.

'I can give you a matchbox for twenty bucks. That do ya?'

One thing about Pug, if you ask, you buy — no room for hesitation. You nod, your heart racing as you step toward him, clutching the twenty-dollar note in your trembling fingers. He emits an almighty howl. Freezing, your heart leaps into your throat. Nearby fold-out chairs creak and groan as mums and dads crane their necks, curious and concerned, wondering if this will ruin their night.

'Shit,' Pug moans, clutching the fingers of his right hand to his chest. 'You stood on me fuckin' hand.'

You stop breathing; all thoughts of buying grass vanish.

Pug throws his head back and laughs. 'Don't worry, Pommy, it ain't gonna kill me.' He pulls out a matchbox, and your twenty-dollar note vanishes into his pocket.

Taking it with a quick nod, you hurry away.

Danny's voice cuts through the dope haze. 'Bloody hell. I asked if you wanna get out of here.' Pug's bloodstained hand swims into your vision. Startled, sitting up straight. Danny's face replaces Pug's, and you relax.

'Well? What about it? Shall we?'

'Umm, it hasn't started yet.'

Exasperated, he snaps, 'Not from here, not tonight.' Waving his arm in a sweeping motion, 'From this shithole.'

'Go where? How?'

'The other day, I spoke to my sister in Sydney. My aunt's not well. We can go see her.'

'Sydney, uh, s'pose.' Your stomach does barrel rolls. 'What about work?'

'I reckon they'll let us go.'

'Okay.' Lying down again, closing your eyes, praying Pug doesn't reappear.

You're eager to leave Darwin ever since the Vic. But Danny's recent moodiness unsettles you. The thought of him abandoning you in an unfamiliar city sends a sliver of fear down your spine. That fear has been with you for most of your life. Now stronger with each passing day. No matter how much you push it away, the idea of being alone terrifies you.

You know you need something to protect you if he does abandon you. Maybe a knife. A flicker of memory: The Vic. The man. The knife. You shake it off. Maybe things would've turned out differently if you'd had one then.

***

Browsing shop windows in Smith Street, your eyes linger on the polished brass and timber stocks in a gun shop. The man inside gives you a sharp look, shooing you away with a wave.

You glance at the new Woolworths — unlikely they'd have anything. Then you remember the disposal store on Cavanagh Street and a glimmer of hope lifts your spirits. That's where you'll find what you need.

The store is lit by a fly-covered bulb hanging from a frayed cord, casting a sickly yellow glow. The smell of mothballs fills your nose as you push through narrow aisles and squeeze past racks of camouflage jackets and pants. Tents, sleeping bags, pots and pans of all sizes clutter the shelves, but you ignore them — you're low on cash and have only one thing on your mind.

Behind a grimy counter, a man in a Hendrix T-shirt with a grey overcoat over the top flicks through a magazine. He looks up, raising an eyebrow in surprise. Sharp eyes peer from dark sockets, and he quickly tucks the magazine away. You glimpse a woman in black tights holding a whip on the cover. He grins, his breath the scent of mangrove swamps where you go crabbing with friends.

'What... what... what... you... you want?'

'I'm... you got any knives?'

'You... you... uh... scare... scare... of... summit?' He starts picking at a fingernail, as if he's forgotten you're there.

'No.'

He stops picking and sniggers. 'Okay. Look... at the... these.' A skeletal finger taps on the counter. 'That... that's... a... good 'un.' He points to a glossy black sheath. 'It's... a... a Bowie.' Opening the case, he picks it up and caresses it like one might a newborn kitten. His dirt-encrusted fingers trace up and down the blade, thumb oozing a yellow liquid. As he places the knife on the counter it makes a solid *thunk*. Holding it carefully, keeping your fingers away from where his thumb touched it. Its weight gives you a feeling of power. 'How, how much?'

'You... nu... need... a... knife that... that big?' A hooting from deep in his chest. 'If you drop... drop... it... mi... might... cut, cut your thing off.' He gurgles. 'It's, uh... five... fifty.'

'Five or fifty?'

His face changed, mirroring the black sheaf. He stares. 'You... you make, make fun of me?'

Wanting to get away, 'No, no, sorry, I didn't... it's... How, how much did you say?'

'It's fifty-five dollars.'

The stutter is gone.

***

As the sun rose over the horizon, Danny's baby-blue Volkswagen manoeuvres across the rutted ground. He pulls up alongside the caravan. A roof rack holds a jerry can and two spare tyres. He'd sold the Cortina for scrap weeks ago. 'Heap of fuckin' rubbish,' he screams. You never see it again.

Looking at the Volkswagen, wondering about the bull bar. 'Why'd you put that on?'

'Roos.'

You consider for a moment. 'You expecting to hit one?'

Ignoring the comment, glancing at the bag at your feet. 'We're going for three weeks. You know.'

Shrugging, reaching for the boot. 'It's all I got.'

Laughing, Danny points to the front of the car. 'The engine's in the back, stupid. Put it in the front.'

An hour later, the excitement of leaving Darwin unravelled like an old jumper. Resting your head against the window, eyelids lowering at the steady hum of the motor.

You wake with a start as the car slows. Sitting upright, blinking away the sleep, turning to Danny. 'What? What's happened?

He motions with his chin toward the road. You see a solitary figure, with thumb outstretched.

'Thanks for stopping, fellas. I was dying out here.' His voice ragged — a craggy, unshaven face peering from under the brim of an Akubra hat. Sweat drips from his chin, hitting the bitumen with tiny plops. Removing his hat, wiping his brow he shades his eyes, squinting at the blazing sky. 'Yup. This heat will kill a man.'

Danny leans across the passenger seat. 'Where are you going?'

'Home, Sydney,' the stranger says, face creasing into an ample smile.

Danny nods. You clamber out to let the stranger in. He swings his olive duffel bag off his shoulder and sticks out a meaty hand. It envelops yours but, unlike Pug, he doesn't crush it. 'I'm Reg. Pleased to meet youse.'

You push the front seat forward. 'Sorry, it's a bit cramped in the back.'

'No problem. Better than standing in this bloody heat. Where can I stow my gear?'

Danny chimes up, 'Stick it next to you. We'll sort it out later.'

Reg sinks into the seat with a sigh. 'Thanks again fellas. Geez, I could murder a cold one.'

Smiling, Danny pulls back onto the highway.

You turn around to face Reg, keen to know more about him. 'How'd you end up hitchhiking all the way out here?'

Grunting, as if the memory is not a pleasant one. With a sniff, 'I was at the rodeo and the blokes with me got fed up with the heat. They decided to leave, bloody city slickers. I stayed. You fellas on holiday?'

Danny nods. 'We're visiting my sister in Sydney.'

A booming laugh from Reg. 'A couple of country boys off to the big smoke.' He snorts, amused by his own humour. 'If youse don't mind, I'm gonna get some shut-eye. That heat took it outta me.'

It's not long before there's a rumbling from the back seat. Looking across at Danny. 'You gonna take him all the way to Sydney?'

Danny shakes his head. 'I dunno. We can. If he doesn't mind helping out.'

Reg's sleepy voice mutters, as much to himself as to Danny, 'I'm happy to help if youse want.'

Laughing, you look over your shoulder. 'Thought you were asleep.'

He smiles, eyes closed.

Turning back to Danny, 'So where we gonna stop and sleep tonight?'

Reg snorts. 'Under the stars, son. Lots of places to lie down. It's a big country.' He begins humming softly to himself.

You begin to understand why Reg ended up on his own. 'We don't have sleeping bags.'

He snickers as if it's a joke. 'We'll work it out. Shit I'm buggered.' He shifts position, the seat groans in protest, five minutes later loud snoring fills the car. The trip has become more interesting.

'We should stop here, this is the best spot we've seen,' Reg nods toward a truckie lay-by. 'We can make a fire. That'll keep nosey critters at a distance.'

You want to ask what he's referring to, but think better of it.

Reg, whistling a tune, heads off to find firewood and returns with an armful of twigs and branches. 'This'll get us started.' Removing his shirt, reveals a chest reddened by the sun and peeling skin on his shoulders. Grunting, he digs a hole between the cracked and soot-blackened bricks. The scent of earth mingles with the sharp smell of burning wood as the fire crackles into life.

'That's impressive Reg.'

He laughs, shakes the box of matches in his hand. 'Gotta have a Redhead.'

You smile and stand alongside him, the flame's heat warming your face, watching the embers float into the darkening sky, their glow fading as they rise. The sound of the fire blends with the distant drone of cicadas, creating a comforting background. Stars come out and twinkle in the dark sky. Reg unrolls his sleeping bag, and familiar snores fill the air. You fall into a fitful slumber, disturbed by passing road trains and the distant yipping of dingoes.

As you toss and turn, you have no idea how important the day's events are. If you did, you might not have slept.

Reflection: The Father Wound

"An absent father can lead to a lifetime of seeking approval and love." — Unknown

A positive male figure is essential for a child's security. However, a father's role is more than providing food and shelter. He guides our emotional development and how to navigate life. Without this, we struggle to form a sense of our own identity. With an absent father, even one that is still within the home, we grow up feeling abandoned and unworthy. Children often blame themselves for their father's neglect or absence even though they have no control over it.

Because we feel unwanted, we create a false self, hoping this false self is worthy of love. We chase validation, sometimes to the point of enduring or inviting abuse. It also makes it difficult to form relationships. We live with a constant underlying feeling of sadness from a father who didn't care emotionally about us. We may have never felt his loving arm around us or heard they were proud of us. We can also attract partners who replicate the emotional neglect or abuse we experienced as a child because it feels familiar. The reaction to having an absent father is different for all of us.

Adult Reaction: Absent Father

I still ache for a father who showed me love or offered a kind word. It never happened. If your experiences are similar, you may have a similar ache. As adults we hesitate to discuss our lack of love from our fathers. Society expects us to be past these emotional responses. But we aren't because we have yet to process the trauma.

My lack of a father figure drove me into the arms of people I believed would protect me. In Pug, I found somebody who had the same violent tendencies as my father. But he made me feel safe. It is often how our lack of a father figure shows up. If someone shows interest in us, we attach ourselves to them as they offer what we failed to receive in childhood: stability and security. I remember wanting to do everything possible to remain with Danny. When he suggested a trip away, my greatest fear was that I'd be alone again if I didn't go. I experienced great joy in leaving Darwin, but I realise that I've been running ever since.

The father wound also makes us believe that the world is dangerous. We see danger everywhere. My fears began to overwhelm me when I was leaving Darwin. That fear took precedence over common sense, leading me to buy the knife, which led to more trouble.

For most of my life I've felt like an outsider. The feeling was so strong that it ended my marriage. I recall the look on my ex-wife's face when I told her I didn't belong in the marriage. She said I was being silly. But the feeling persisted, so I packed up and left. I realise how ridiculous I sounded. But, it's how deeply the father wound affects us. It also made me a poor parent. I left my children when they were young. I know this caused them hurt and pain. Because we learn from childhood experience — which for me was one of neglect and abandonment — we distance ourselves from our children. We need to be aware that all they want is love and attention. If we do this, it will help them to become emotionally healthy, well-balanced adults — an opportunity I didn't have.

I am still moved to sadness, even tears, when I see a fatherly figure on television or in a movie hugging their son. However, I've come to realise that healing takes time and patience. Let's explore how we heal from the father wound.

Healing Exercise: Letter Writing

Healing starts with acknowledging the impact of an absent father on our lives. We need to recognise it for what it is — neglect, abandonment and abuse. Explore the depth of your father wound to know how it drives your emotions and wants. It's important not to lay blame; remember, our fathers faced abuse too. It's about understanding and reflecting on our childhood experiences rather than judgment.

Most importantly, we must remember that we are not our fathers. What happened to us was not our fault. But healing is our responsibility.

In the following exercise, we'll discover what our inner child feels and wants from us. Get paper and a pen, then find a quiet spot. Close your eyes and take several deep breaths. Imagine your inner child is in front of you. Open your eyes and write a letter to it using your dominant hand, i.e., if right-handed, use your right hand. We use the dominant hand, because it's most closely connected to our present. Tell your inner child how sorry you are for the treatment it received. Let it know you're here to provide support, love and protection. Add anything else that is necessary. Then, take a few more deep breaths.

This time, we'll write back to our adult selves from our inner child. Using our non-dominant hand, which is more closely connected to our unconscious mind, where our emotions reside, lets the thoughts and feelings flow, capturing everything. How did it feel then? How does it feel now? What would it like from you? When finished, carefully consider both letters. What is your inner child saying? How can you help it heal?

Mine wanted to be hugged, to feel my love. It asked why it wasn't loved and if it was bad. Repetition is vital in connecting with our inner child. I recommend spending a few minutes every day talking to it.

When undertaking any of these exercises, it's also essential to take care of yourself. If they bring up too much trauma, stop and seek professional help. I also recommend finding an activity that helps you relax: painting, pottery, singing, playing a musical instrument or spending time in nature.

As my connection to Danny crumbled, I realised he wasn't a good father figure. But I was terrified of being alone. Reg made me feel more secure. However, it became unhealthy, as I was desperate to please him at every opportunity. This longing for approval often reveals itself as a need to please others. We'll examine this pattern more deeply in the next chapter as we explore how people-pleasing shapes adult lives.

Chapter Eight

Walking on Eggshells

The sign reads 'ELCOME TO EENSLAND'. Bullet holes obliterated the 'W'. Whoever did the shooting was either good or up close, likely the latter. The 'Q' and 'U' are gone too. A shit-encrusted cattle grid is the only other clue that you're entering another state.

Disappointed, you turn to Reg. 'How much further?'

Reg inclines his head and winks. 'We'll be in Mount Isa tonight, then it's a hop, skip and jump.' Chuckling, he gets back in the car.

After miles of dusty red plains, Reg has a suggestion. 'How about trying some of the local brew?'

Danny, with a shake of his head, insists we keep going. 'Need to make Mount Isa.'

Reg, in a quiet voice, 'You're on holiday, relax.'

To take Reg's mind off a cold drink — if that's possible, you ask, 'Reg, it's barren out here, why'd you leave if you like it so much?'

He doesn't answer for a while, and you turn around to see if he's dropped off to sleep. Deep in thought, he stirs. 'I dunno. Being in the bush makes me happy. I spent years out here as a ringer, when I was about your age, Graham, maybe a bit older.' He hesitates, then continues. 'Real friendly people, hardworking decent folk. Do anything for you if you're genuine. They don't suffer fools.' He stops, lost in memories, sadness flits across his face.

Wanting to leave him to his thoughts, but you can't resist one more question. 'What's a ringer?'

Laughing, he said, 'They muster cattle, Graham. The big properties have thousands of 'em. I enjoyed that time. The bush in early mornings. A silvery mist in the air. The only sound, distant calls of waking birds. When the mist lifts, it leaves behind a bright blue cloudless sky. I got no truck with religion, but you gotta believe in something bigger than yourself when you're out here. It gives you a sense of being insignificant yet also part of it. The stars in an inky black sky are remarkable, too. The way they twinkle and dance puts the first cold beer to shame.'

Smiling, 'A bit of a poet, are you?'

'Nah. A simple bushy.'

You persist. 'Why aren't you still working as a ringer?'

Reg sighs. 'It's hard yakka.' Laughing, 'Anyway, I got me dream job. Working in a brewery.' He licks his lips and swallows. 'Speaking of which…'

You ignore the last part, knowing Danny is not going to stop. 'What did you eat out here?'

Reg grins. 'Whatever I could shoot. Plenty on the hoof out here.'

You consider what might be edible. Not much comes to mind. 'Rabbits?'

A choking sound from Reg. 'Rabbits! You can't eat them. They're crook. Roos you can, but gotta check for worms.' Now regretting you asked, but Reg is on a roll. 'Of course, there's camel, if you can develop a taste for it. I couldn't. I like juicy steaks. The stuff you're used to, Graham.'

Outraged, you snap, 'I've eaten other stuff. I've eaten a snake.'

Reg holds up his hands. 'Whoa. I didn't mean anything.' Grinning, 'How did you end up eating a snake?' Annoyed, you remain silent. 'C'mon, tell us.'

Danny concentrates on the road and doesn't join the conversation.

Taking a deep breath, you want Reg to like you. Having him along has taken the pressure off your relationship with Danny.

Soothed, you continue. 'When I was young, we lived in Africa.'

Reg cackles. 'You're young now.'

Looking over your shoulder, giving him a hard look. He grins. 'I had it then. Me and a friend were camping. We wanted to cook mealie maize.'

Reg pipes up, 'That's not a snake.'

This time you give him a dirty look. 'You wanna hear or not?' He nods, a look of innocence crosses his face.

'We needed a tin of Carnation milk for the maize. To get to the closest shop, we had to walk along a dirt track past a chicken coop.' You pause, remembering how close you came to being bitten. 'Anyway, we're walking back, and there's rustling in the grass near the coop. A snake darts through a gap in the chicken-wire fence, but it dislodges a rock and gets trapped, stopping an inch from my ankle.' You shiver remembering the day. 'My friend, with a yell that would scare a lion, whips out a machete and chops the snake's head off. Then we cooked it.'

Reg is quiet. 'Any idea what sort of snake? Poisonous?'

You shrug. 'No idea. My friend said with the head gone, it would be okay.'

Reg leans forward. 'You like it?'

'I can't remember much, other than it was chewy.'

Settling back into his seat, 'Sorry Graham, shouldn't have doubted you.'

A silence descends on the car as we pass open plains dotted with silvery Mallee trees and scrubby grass, desolate but beautiful. You begin to understand Reg's love of this place. Reg, meanwhile, clears his throat as you pass each town, making a loud smacking noise with his lips, then staring mournfully out of the rear window as they disappeared in a cloud of red dust.

Unable to hold his tongue any longer, 'If we can't stop for a drink, what about a shower and clean sheets?'

The comment hangs in the air, but the unease remains. You felt annoyed by Reg's teasing. You were back facing your father, waiting for approval and again failing to measure up. Swallowing your annoyance, the thought of upsetting Reg was too much. You wanted him to like you. Perhaps then, things would improve with Danny. The tension between him and Reg was growing, and you're desperate to ensure it doesn't explode. *One wrong word, and he'll leave me.* Staring out the window at the endless stretch of dry earth. *What if I tell him how I feel?* A shake of your head. You didn't have that kind of courage.

Danny's lips formed a thin line. 'Where are you thinking, Reg?'

'How about Brisbane? I've a friend there. Youse can go and check out Surfer's for a coupla days. It's a good place to meet sheilas.' He laughs and thumps the back of your seat, sending you headfirst into the dash. 'Oops, sorry Graham,' patting you on the shoulder.

You rub your forehead, hoping it isn't split open. 'You got a girl, Reg?'

Shaking his head, 'Nah. But we're getting crabby cooped up in this tin can. It might do us all good.' Staring at the back of Danny's head.

'We could do with a break. What do you think?' Surprisingly, he nods in agreement. With no argument, even though he's spent the entire trip rushing to get to Sydney. *What's on his mind?* You find out soon enough.

As you get closer to Brisbane, the tension between Danny and Reg reaches boiling point.

In relief, Reg points to a group of shops near the highway. 'Drop me off here. Surfer's is about an hour further on.' Grabbing his bag, taking your elbow, he leads you away from the car. 'You won't leave without me, will you? I enjoy travelling with youse.'

'No. Of course not.'

'Okay. Get a motel, past Surfer's, otherwise it'll cost you an arm and a leg.' He leaves with a slap on your back, a wink and a parting quip. 'Stay outta trouble and I'll see youse back here in three days?'

***

Reg is pacing up and down in front of the shops as you pull up. He waves, hurrying over. 'Great to see you. Youse had me worried.'

You're pleased to see him as well. You considered mentioning that Danny wanted to leave him behind, but decided against it, seeing his relief.

'Did you have a good time, Reg?' He nods, wiping his brow with a handkerchief as he struggles into the back seat. 'You putting on weight?'

Brushing off the comment. 'It was fine.' Tell me about youse. Did you go to Surfer's? Meet any sheilas?'

You smile. Danny grimaces.

You'd argued about whether to tell Reg what happened. Danny insisted you shouldn't, but you thought it was hilarious.

Danny groaned, 'That's the problem. He will, too, and we'll never hear the end of it.'

You couldn't resist, knowing Reg would savour every detail.

By the time you finish, Reg is holding his belly, gurgling with delight, while Danny glares daggers at you. Reg snorts, handkerchief in hand, wiping tears from his eyes. 'Let me get this straight,' he says, still chuckling. 'You met two girls, backpackers. That right?' His face goes a shade of blue as another fit of giggles takes hold. Taking a breath, regaining his composure, in a solemn voice, as if explaining something of the utmost importance to a child, 'They liked you, right?'

You nod, enjoying this. Danny grips the steering wheel, his face a blank mask.

'So, these girls become more interested in youse when they find out you're staying in a motel. That correct?'

You don't answer, knowing there's more.

'These girls, they ask about the laundry and then disappear without a word after they wash their clothes, is that right?' The car fills with his belly laugh. You're concerned he might be having a heart attack as he presses his hands against his chest, roaring. 'And, and,' gasping, 'Youse wait for them to finish.' Tears run down his cheeks as he splutters like a newborn baby.

'They said they wouldn't be long, Reg.' He's having too much fun at your expense and you're beginning to regret telling him.

Danny turns to you. 'I warned you.'

Reg ignores him. 'Didn't I tell youse to be careful? I suggested local sheilas, not backpackers. Gawd almighty. So now the best dressed backpackers in this country are in Queensland, that's great.' He collapses into high-pitched giggles.

'Shut up Reg,' struggling to hold back a smile.

∗∗∗

You cross the Queensland border into New South Wales, with no fanfare. You don't even see any signs. The country changes to endless rows of green stalks.

'Sugar cane,' Reg says. 'It's big out here. Hard work cutting…' an air horn blasts, interrupting him, as a cattle truck speeds past. The car, buffeted by the wind, sways from side to side. Danny fights with the steering wheel. Reg mutters, 'Geez. He's in a hurry.'

CRACK.

The windscreen explodes.

'Fuck.' Danny yells. Reg screams for him to pull over, his hands grip the rear of your seat. Danny stops the car and rests his forehead on the steering wheel, moaning, 'Bloody hell.'

You stare at the hole where the windscreen used to be, shocked at how little remains. Tiny shards of glass sprinkle into your lap as you run your hands through your hair. Thankfully, your hands come away without blood; relieved, you shake your head, dislodging more glass into your lap.

'You okay, Reg? Danny?' you ask, steadying your voice. Danny's face is ashen as he stares at the damage.

Reg taps your arm. 'C'mon. We can't sit here. Let's clean it up.'

'But it's smashed to pieces. Can we still make it to Sydney?'

Danny mumbles, 'Hope it doesn't rain.' On cue, a rumble of thunder splits the sky. Glancing skyward, you see dark clouds gathering in the distance.

Reg nods. 'They get big storms in these parts. Better get moving.'

The air is warm, but you shiver as it blows through the car, pulling your shirt tight around your shoulders, huddling below the dash to escape the wind. The noise hurts your eardrums. 'You okay back there, Reg?' A muffled response. He's wrapped his coat around his head like a Bedouin fighter. Danny faces the worst of it — he has to withstand the wind in his face, his brow creases as he peers out of the window. Raindrops plop onto the bonnet. Your chest tightens. *Rain is all we need.* You glance at the sky, fearing worse to come.

Above the din of the wind, Reg shouts, 'There's a garage ahead. They might have something to cover it and stop this bloody wind.'

Danny nods and pulls in alongside a Golden Fleece pump, red with rust. 'You reckon that's working?'

Reg shrugs. 'We'll find out.' He gets out, stretching and groaning, 'Geez, I'll be glad when we arrive in Sydney.' He disappears inside the shop; you hear a door bang.

Danny studies the darkening sky. The rain has held off, but he looks worried. 'You, okay?'

'Some holiday. This'll set me back a bit.' Worried that Danny will turn around and go back to Darwin, you try to cheer him up, offering to pay.

Reg returns, holding something aloft like a trophy. 'These places carry everything. I got this. The bloke said the town's not far from here. We should be able to get the screen replaced in the morning.' Danny frowns. Reg whistles as he fits the plastic screen in place, almost as if to annoy Danny. 'Trap the end of the plastic in the door, and we'll be sweet.'

Danny mutters, 'Bloody hell, it's hard to see.' He pulls onto the highway. 'I'm as blind as a bat.' You close your eyes, hoping the town isn't far.

BANG.

The car shoots forward like a bullet from a gun, sliding across the road. Tyres screech as Danny brakes, desperately trying to keep it from careening into a ditch at the side of the road. Frightened, you don't know what's happened. Reg is swearing. Danny screams, 'What the...?'

The car's front wheel is in the ditch. Worried the car might slip further into the ditch, you get out with great care, the freed plastic flaps in the wind.

A car is stationary in the centre of the road, headlights blazing, and four young men, not much older than boys, are standing beside it.

One, near the driver's door moves towards you, a sneer on his face, his hands balled into fists. 'Why'd you pull out in front of us like that?'

Reg exhales. 'Hang on a minute, son. You hit us in the rear. We were in the middle of the bloody road.'

'You reckon?' He raises his hands. Dropping them, as he glances over his shoulder at an approaching blue flashing light. Turning back, he sneers, 'You're bloody lucky.'

He walks away as the police car comes to a halt, and an officer struggles out, pulling his belt up over a large beer belly. Straightening his jacket, he marches towards you.

'What's happened here? Anyone hurt?'

The boy, now with his hands in his pockets, says, 'They caused it.'

The officer glares at him and repeats his question. 'Is anyone hurt?' The four shake their heads. We do the same. 'All right, what happened?'

The boy mutters sullenly, 'They pulled out in front of us. I couldn't miss 'em.' The officer gives him another hard stare. 'You're Charlie Pearson's boy, Ed, ain't you?'

A wicked grin spread across his face. 'Yeah. Look, it's their fault.' The officer unclips a torch, shining it over the boy's car. A dent marks the centre of the chrome bumper. He shuffles to the Volkswagen, inspecting large dents in both the bumper and boot, then peers into the interior. *Shit, the trip to Sydney is over.*

'They hit us,' Reg insists. 'Are you the driver?' Reg shakes his head, nodding towards Danny.

'Alright. I want a word over here. Ed, you and your friends, be quiet and get out of the middle of the bloody road.'

Reg whispers, 'I've got a bad feeling about this. We're in trouble.'

The officer returns still struggling with his belt, his belly winning the battle. Danny trails behind, looking like he's eaten a bad prawn. The officer, hands on hips, surveys the four boys and then you.

'You're not going much further tonight. The fellas at our local garage can work on the car overnight. Meanwhile, we'll offer you some country hospitality.'

'What about the damage? Who'll pay?' Reg asks, motioning to the boys.

'I'll look into it. They say you pulled out in front of them. That piece of plastic would have made your vision difficult.' He turns to the boys. 'Ed, is your car okay to drive?'

Ed looks despondent, you're positive he's hoping you'd all spend the night in jail. Dragging the toe of one shoe on the road, he mutters, 'I guess.'

'I reckon you've all had enough for one night. Go home. I'll talk to your parents' tomorrow.'

As a tow truck arrives, you realise this may not be the first accident on this part of the highway. Danny, eyes downcast, sits in front. Reg, on the other hand, grins from ear to ear and licks his lips in anticipation when the officer says the accommodation is at the local pub.

The publican's face contorts with irritation. 'What do you mean I'm putting them up for the night?' he growls, his smile forced.

'I'll make sure it's taken care of,' snaps the officer.

The publican, with a defiant scowl, wanders off, muttering about his good nature being taken advantage of — not that you've seen much evidence of that nature.

Reg heads to the bar, ordering a beer for himself and Danny. 'Lemon squash for you, Graham?' Reg raises his glass. 'Cheer up, fellas. Could be worse; we could've been hurt, but here we are having a beer.' He signals for another.

The publican moans loud enough for everyone to hear, lamenting that he'll be out on the street if this keeps up.

Reg downs his second beer in two gulps. 'Let's have dinner, get some sleep, and, as they say in the classics, the rest will take care of itself.'

'I know what's going to happen. Nothing,' Danny mutters.

'You're right. The quicker we leave, the better. Those boys are locals, and the copper knows their parents. Whatever we say won't matter.'

'Yeah, but that means we'll have to pay for the damage.'

'That's better than paying for both. And that could happen.'

***

The officer returns early the following day, his uniform freshly pressed, and three stripes on his sleeve.

You feel uncomfortable this close to a police officer. You recall other times with police and it had never worked out well. Your stomach has a hollow feeling at the thought of having to challenge authority. You just wanted everything to be as it was before the accident.

'I've spoken to the mechanic. He's been working on your car, so you should be on your way shortly. The good news is the motor's okay. He'll put a new screen on, too.'

Danny, jaw clenched, 'What about the ones who hit us? Are they going to pay for it?'

The officer stands tall, though still a foot shorter than Danny and stares up at him. 'I've got conflicting stories, faults on both sides, so I reckon we call it even and move on. After all, we took care of you last night.'

Watching Danny's face, Reg steps in, interrupting before he says something regrettable. 'Thank you, officer. It's appreciated.'

Not a word is exchanged during the trip to the garage. Each of us lost in our own thoughts. Danny's mind is likely on the money. Yours on getting to Sydney. Reg has a satisfied smile on his face. You assume he's thinking about last night's beer.

The officer calls out to a man working on the rear of the car, he pokes his head around the side. 'This is a tough beast. There's nothing damaged on the motor. I replaced the screen.'

Reg nods. 'How much?'

The mechanic scratches his behind and sneaks a look at the officer, who gives a slight nod. 'A couple of hundred will see you good.'

The officer walks away and leans against his car.

You whisper to Reg. 'Can we do anything?'

Reg shakes his head. 'Those young fellas had a beer or two in 'em, is my guess. You look after locals, not strangers, in these towns. He's going to make damn sure they're okay.'

You and Reg chip in to help Danny pay for the repairs, but it does little to ease his mood. As you leave, the officer follows. 'Like a good 'ol sheriff,' Reg mutters.

You relax, knowing your problems are behind you. The beginnings of a smile on your lips as you look forward to Sydney. You should've known better.

Reflection: People-Pleasing

"To be selfless, you must first have a self that you can give up. There is a world of difference between giving up yourself and giving up on your self."
— Eugene Terekhin

People-pleasing is about seeking approval from others and questioning our worth when we don't get it. We put others' needs, opinions, and feelings before our own. Our self-worth becomes based on what others think of us. People-pleasing is tied closely to the father wound.

Emotionally absent caregivers or those who have conflict within the home drive us to find peace as children even when it is not within our capability to do so.

As people-pleasers, we have great difficulty with confrontation or conflict. It's safer to remain mute rather than voice our opinion, especially if it is different from others, as it could be criticised. We are easily manipulated to do things others may not want to do.

We rarely express our own opinions, preferring to wait to see which way a conversation goes and then agree even if we secretly disagree. We laugh at jokes that are not funny and smile at things that are against our values and morals. All of this is because we have a deep need to be accepted. We learnt in childhood that this is our safe option.

We'll apologise when we've done nothing to apologise for. We assume we are wrong no matter the situation. My trauma has impacted me to the point where I see myself as subservient in almost every situation. When I worked with young graduates in the public service I often felt they knew more and were more capable than I was.

We can put ourselves into dangerous situations to prove we are courageous. All the while, our inner child is terrified. People-pleasing also means we will suppress feelings of resentment or frustration until we reach a breaking point, often leading to an emotional explosion. It's all about the desire for acceptance and approval because we lacked that as a child. We do everything possible to gain that acceptance and approval. If any of this feels familiar, then know you have people-pleasing tendencies.

Adult Reaction: Connection

As adults, we find ourselves agreeing with everyone to ensure their happiness and peace — at the cost of our own happiness. We become incapable of saying no, as we want to be seen as always ready to help. All of this equates to our absolute fear of abandonment and rejection.

I gravitated towards older men who might fill the emptiness left by the lack of love from my father. To ensure they would like me, I would people-please and do anything asked of me. Reg embodied what I wanted in a father. Someone who gave me attention, listened and showed interest in what I said and did. For him, it appeared a natural, friendly reaction. For me, it was about missing those emotional bonds as a child and desperately wanting them.

We yearn for acceptance and love and do everything possible to be part of a group and receive approval.

Our wounded inner child is very aware of nonverbal cues about how to behave. In the early eighties, I attended the opening of a nightclub in Sydney. It was going to be a popular night spot, and although I didn't feel I belonged in that social environment, I wanted to go and be part of it. So, I bought the current trend in clothes: parachute pants and a tight-fitting knitted top. I looked ridiculous. I felt like a fraud, which I was. I left an hour after I arrived.

Around the same time, I hung out with a group of people who were gay. I pretended that I was gay, too, acting and dressing accordingly so they'd accept me.

We also anticipate the needs and requirements of people we come in contact with. I'll walk into a room and look for someone I can converse with. If I find them, I rarely approach anyone else. This occurs because we focus on external validation. All of our inner child wounds are linked to our original childhood trauma of not being loved. If we could wave a magic wand, the only request would be to be loved.

Healing Exercise: Validating Ourselves

The long-term effects of people-pleasing include anxiety, chronic stress, low self-esteem and a loss of personal identity. Learning to recognise these patterns is crucial to healing and establishing healthy relationships.

Healing from any trauma is a journey that requires dedication and commitment. We can heal our people-pleasing tendencies by delving into the memories of when we first felt unloved and the pain we experienced.

Consider your relationship with your caregivers. Did you feel safe? Could you express your feelings without fear? Now, imagine a life without people-pleasing. Think of expressing genuine feelings to someone and embracing your true self. Ultimately, we must understand our worth is not tied to someone else's value or their approval.

Here is an exercise you can do daily to improve your self-worth. The words we say to ourselves and others are powerful. Each morning, ask what changes you could make — or need to make — to demonstrate self-respect. Would it be speaking up in a meeting? Being honest in a response if someone says something you disagree with? Remind yourself that you are valued. Walk with your head held high and your shoulders back. Show the world that you are proud. As you do, you'll grow confident and realise you no longer rely on others to make you feel worthy.

Arriving in Sydney should have been a fresh start. Instead, my people-pleasing continued to shape my relationships. It was as if my worth depended on keeping everyone happy. The moment I experienced another loss, my fear of abandonment took over. The abandonment wound isn't a fear of being alone. It's the terror of being invisible. Next, we explore how deeply abandonment affects us and how it drives good and bad adult decision-making.

Chapter Nine

Silent Goodbye

A giant hand opened a magical jewelled box. That's your impression as you cross Sydney Harbour Bridge. Sunlight glitters against office windows, casting dazzling beams across the harbour. Ferries chugged across a pea-green-coloured water, white foam at their bows. One word summed it up: Home.

'Take the Cahill,' Reg's fist slamming into the rear of the seat to make his point.

Danny jockeys the car into the correct lane as you sweep down the expressway.

Ahead is a building covered in scaffolding, resembling the conch shells you searched for on Hunstanton Beach. Over your shoulder, 'Reg, what's that?'

His eyes sparkle. 'That's an opera house. Or it will be.' Then, with a quick shake of his head. 'A waste of money, if you ask me.' His hand smacks your seat again. 'Turn, here, here!'

Danny veers across another lane, drivers honk their horns in annoyance.

'Follow this road, then turn left at Pitt Street. I'll show you.'

The sun disappears behind the buildings as you wind your way through the city, crowds rush to wherever they are going, none raise their heads to look at a dirt-coated Volkswagen.

People's Palace, here we come. You smile to yourself.

***

On the way into Sydney, Danny pulled over at a payphone to call his sister.

You watch his jaw tighten, his voice carrying through the glass booth. He slams the handset down, marching back to the car. His face is a mask of frustration.

Reg caught your eye. A shake of his head urged you to stay silent.

Danny gets in and smacks his hand on the dashboard. 'Bloody hell. We have to change plans.' Your heart sank at his words.

'My sister's got a job and is staying at the YWCA in the city.'

'What? Why's that a problem?'

A guffaw from behind you. 'Can't stay there, it's only for girls. You won't get through the front door.'

Danny sniffed. 'Thanks Reg, I know.'

'Can we stay with your aunt?'

Shaking his head, 'The rest of her family has turned up and she's got no room for us. That's why my sister moved.'

Flinching from the anger in his voice, 'We're on holiday. We'll be okay.'

Frowning, Danny snaps, 'I'm nearly broke. The car...' He raised his hand as if to strike the dash again. 'This is turning out to be a shit holiday.'

'I know a place near the YWCA,' said Reg. 'Run by the Salvos, it's pretty cheap. Umm, it's... oh yeah, People's Palace. A bit dodgy.' The implication hung in the air.

Blushing, 'I can take care of myself.'

Reg nodded. 'Sure, sure, you can.'

Turning to Danny. 'Let's check it out. No harm staying a night or two.'

***

It seemed reasonable then, but now, doubt gnawed at you, as you look at the dishevelled building. Danny frowns, breaking the silence. 'You sure it's got accommodation, Reg? Doesn't look much like a palace.'

Reg chuckles, a sound that doesn't quite match the unease in his eyes. 'No, a palace it ain't, but it's better than the one over there.' He nods towards a building on the opposite side of the street. Neon lights blink, casting a faint glow above a grimy entrance. A sign read, 'Rooms to let.' A man in a drab grey overcoat sits on the steps, rocking back and forth on his heels. He stares into the distance, oblivious to the passers-by who avoid him.

Reg's voice drops, a hint of warning in his words. 'That one's cheaper. But I wouldn't recommend it.'

Danny glanced across, then back to the People's Palace. 'This one doesn't look much better.'

Reg snorts, poking Danny in the shoulder. 'Go round the corner, Campbell Street. That'll do me.' He gets out, inhales and shakes his head. 'I miss this place when I'm away. Appreciate the lift, fellas.' He looks you in the eye. 'If you need me, I'll be at the Bellevue pub. Come say g'day. It's near Redfern Station. Remember that, Graham. Bellevue.'

'Um, okay,' even though you don't expect to see him again.

He laughs. 'Make sure you do.' Hefting his duffel bag onto his shoulder, he waves, then walks away, sweat-stained Akubra perched at an angle.

You watch him go with a pang of loss. Then, with a shrug, 'C'mon, let's check out this place and catch up with your sister.'

Danny nods. 'I guess.' He strides away.

The man on the steps continues to rock on his heels.

Danny glances at you, then goes up the stairs and into the People's Palace.

Voices drift through an open door leading into a café, accompanied by the clinking of cutlery. A glass-fronted booth in the lobby centre reminds you of a ticket box at a circus. Inside, watching you approach, is a large woman. She looks at you in disdain. A pronounced sniff as if something terrible is assaulting her senses. Sweat glistens between the rolls of neck fat, close-set eyes filled with distrust scrutinise you. She raises a hand and adjusts her bun, never breaking her piercing gaze.

Danny smiles. 'We'd like a room, please.'

With a cold laugh, 'For how long?'

'Uh, tonight...'

'One night.' She cackles, bringing to mind witches and boiling pots. 'This isn't a doss house. There's a minimum five-night stay. And no shared rooms.' She turns away and picks up a book, placing a set of tortoise-shell glasses on her nose, ignoring us. Turning a page, she concentrates on the words.

Stammering, you ask, 'How, how much for... for five nights?'

There's a pause, then, running her finger along the edge of a page, bending a corner to mark her place, she closes the book with a snap, followed by an exaggerated sigh. 'A hundred dollars for five nights.' She places the book on the counter; you sneak a look at the cover. You can make out one word, Portnoy's. She notices, bristling, with upper lip twitching, she slides it off the counter. 'Do you want the rooms or not?'

'Um, uh, yes, we do. We will,' Danny says.

'There's one on the first floor, the other is on the third. You're not allowed on the women's or family floors. There's a television room on the third floor. No television after nine at night.' She announces this in a voice reminiscent of a school principal, then places two pieces of paper and a pen in a tray at the bottom of the glass. 'Fill these out.'

The room is barely big enough for you to stretch your arms without your fingernails scraping against either wall. Worn and cracked linoleum covers the floor. A cupboard and a single iron bed are the only furnishings. A towel and a bar of Palmolive soap on the bed. Bed springs squeak and the mattress dips as you lie down, resting your feet on the end rail.

Sighing in pleasure, *Shit, I'm in Sydney*. You can't believe it.

***

Waiting out the front of the YWCA, pumping your chest out, glancing in the window to admire your new buckskin vest — *it suits me. Where is she?*

A woman inside, an unfriendly look on her face. Moving out of sight, glad the jacket hides the worst of your tattered shirt, though not the fraying collar or sleeves.

You recall the salesman's face when you said you'd wear it out of the shop. 'Excuse me Sir, you don't want it in a bag, is that correct, Sir?'

'I'm gonna wear it now.'

An expression of horror, hands fluttering, then with an effort, he regathered himself. 'Uh, oh, very well. Should I leave the price tag on Sir?' You miss the sarcasm. He rummages in a drawer, pulling out a pair of pink-handled scissors. Mumbling to himself, he cuts off the tag, handing you a bag with 'Farmers' on it. 'Just in case, Sir,' he says, turning his back.

***

Turning your mind to Danny's sister. *How do you tell her he's not coming? Will she blame you?* Smacking your hand against your thigh. *Damn it.*

The first meeting with Lisa does not go as expected. She is waiting on the steps of the YWCA, arms folded across her chest.

If Danny expects a warm welcome, he is disappointed.

She rolls her eyes. 'You two could do with a shower.' A wisp of auburn hair blows across her face; a flick of her fingers and it is gone. She continues 'Hmm. I can't invite you in, you know.'

Danny, in an icy voice, 'Nice to see you too, sis.'

Your heart pounds as you look at her brown eyes, specks of green glint in the fading light.

Raising her hand, she barks, 'I'm tired, I've gotta work early. But you can come back tomorrow night and we'll go for drinks. Some friends of mine will be there, so be nice, brother.' She studies you, the faint beginnings of a blush on your face. 'Are you old enough to get into a pub?'

Nodding, 'Yes, I am, I mean...' dropping your gaze as if you were back in high school.

'Okay. See you at seven. And clean yourselves up.' Spinning on her heel, she walks back inside.

Danny, red-faced and irritated, trudges back towards the Palace.

'Is she always like that?'

'Yeah. We don't get on.'

'No kidding.'

The next night didn't go well either. Danny and Lisa didn't speak to each other. He scowled at her friends. Whenever the conversation turned to the trip or Darwin, his replies were curt and dismissive, and they gave up, ignoring us.

Lisa, as we left, perhaps to make amends, invited us to a party. 'It'll be fun. Might help if you're more pleasant, brother.'

The next day, driving back from Danny's aunt's place, you try to convince him to go. His fist strikes the steering wheel. 'She doesn't care. I say we leave.'

'I wanna stay.'

Eyes bulging, face contorted in rage, he shouts, 'I don't care. I need your money to get home.'

'Go then.' You hurl a handful of notes at him; he stuffs them into his pocket. Slamming the car door, you storm back to the Palace. In your room, you count out what's left.

Shit, one hundred and sixty five dollars. FUCK!

***

'Where is he?'

Her voice catches you by surprise. Turning, your mouth drops open. A green silk top wraps tightly around her full breasts. Her eyes watch yours as your face heats up.

'He's your brother. You know how he is.'

She wipes a hand across her brow as if swatting away an annoying fly. 'His loss. It'll be fun tonight.'

'Why? What's happening?'

She winks. 'Wait and find out. Is that a new jacket?'

'Yeah, great, isn't it?'

'If you say so. C'mon, let's go. We gotta get a cab. The party's in Bondi.'

Deflated, running your fingers down the length of the jacket. *What's wrong with it?*

Lisa waves down a cab, gives directions and settles into her seat. You're enjoying being with her, glad Danny isn't there. Clamping your hands against your thighs, avoiding an accidental touching of her leg, smiling to yourself — *maybe not so accidentally* — she stares out the window, oblivious to the raging heat inside you.

The cab driver also watches her in the rear-vision mirror, following her every move. But if she's aware, there's no indication. Stopping outside a high-rise block of flats, stepping onto streets, slick and shiny from recent rain, you pull your vest tight to beat back the wind. The sound of waves breaking on a nearby beach, a reminder of Fannie Bay.

Grabbing your shoulder, she shouts, 'They live on the top floor. C'mon,' moving you towards the building, her touch bringing another surge of pleasure. *My Girl* blasts out as the door opens, accompanied by a heady smell you recognise.

A bare-chested man with long dreadlocks, a white and yellow sarong around his waist, stands in the doorway. His ebony body shines with sweat and his face cracks into a beaming smile. 'Hey, you made it, crazy,' pulling her into his chest. She wraps her arms around him, they kiss.

Your heart hits the bottom of your feet. Holding his hand, introducing him as Samuel, smiling in a way you haven't seen her do in the short time you've known her.

You're no longer looking forward to the remainder of the night.

'Man, have I got a surprise for jah!' Samuel shouts as we enter. 'Now, my Lisa here...'

He opens a cupboard, its shelves empty apart from a square block no larger than a sugar cube, wrapped in silver foil. Lisa squeals. Hands clapping from those seated in a circle. 'This the best hash anywhere, man. Dem brings it in,' he says, picking it up between his finger and thumb. His next words chill you to the bone: 'Hope dem can handle it.'

He unwraps the block, the girl beside you produces a razor blade and scrapes slivers of hash onto the foil. Someone offers cigarette papers and a tin of tobacco. The girl takes a pinch, lays it on the cigarette paper and sprinkles the hash over the top. She rolls it, twisting and licking both ends, and hands it to Samuel, who lights up. There's a hushed silence as everyone waits their turn. He passes the joint along, greedy fingers waving in the air, waiting for it.

Trembling as if it's a stick of dynamite, you place it between your lips, inhaling, sputtering and coughing. Samuel, a smug look on his face, nodding. Lisa leans forward, her top slipping from one of her ivory shoulders. 'You, okay?'

Eyes fixed on her shoulder, you nod, unable to speak. More joints are passed around. Your lips are numb, head spinning. Lisa's face swims into view, but not the Lisa you know. This one has blazing green eyes and a mouth crammed with rotting teeth.

A loud bang startles you. Someone yells, 'It's cops!'

Panicking, staggering to your feet, mumbling, 'Gotta get out.' Legs shaking like jelly, you sway, unsteady on your feet. *The balcony, go that way.* Grabbing the curtain, your other hand searching for a door handle, you hear loud laughter.

'Stop, stop, dem make a joke,' Samuel cackles. 'Sit.' He's rolling on the floor holding his stomach. Blinking, you look at him, dazed, confused, your grip on the curtain tightening.

Samuel wheezes, eyes lit up with humour. 'You jump?' His belly shakes again.

Stumbling back to the circle, you flop to the floor. Lisa prods you with her foot. 'Are you alright? You don't look good.'

'Uh, I'm, mmm... need, need to...' Lurching to your feet once again, heading for the bathroom, praying it's empty. The toilet bowl is nearly within reach when your stomach erupts, spewing a yellow and green shower across the floor. With a moan, hands covered in slime, head pounding, you rest your cheek against the cool porcelain. Whimpering, you continue to spew. You get up and hobble to the sink, spitting out the dregs. A pale face with red-rimmed eyes stares back at you from the mirror. Tottering to the door, opening a crack to peek into the lounge room. Smoke dribbles from incense sticks jammed into a plant pot. One person is curled up asleep on the floor. There's no sign of Lisa or Samuel. Tiptoeing past the prone body, lying down, you wait for sleep.

Your eyes spring open at the sound of loud voices. Not daring to make a sound, you squeeze them shut, pretending to be asleep. *What could I say?*

Perfume wafts through the room. A skirt rustles, a heel clicking on kitchen tiles. 'At least he cleaned up, not like the other one,' Lisa says, stepping over you. A door bangs shut.

How can I ever face her again?

You fall into a troubled sleep, dreaming of Lisa's green speckled eyes and a smile that grips your heart. The rest is a blur, involving a black man with braided hair.

Bright sunlight pierces your eyelids. Raising your head off the carpet, the stink of vomit and hash in the flat is overwhelming.

Better get back to the Palace. Danny will wonder where I am.

Your worst nightmare unfolds; she's in the booth, sneering, watching you shuffle across the foyer, taking note of each step.

You let out a huge sigh as she looks away.

Your hand holds onto the banister as you stagger to Danny's room.

Catching your breath, rehearsing what you'll say, you knock. No response. Trembling, you had to say the right thing. To make him understand how much you want him to stay in Sydney. Exhausted, leaning against the door, it swung open, staggering into the room, falling flat on your face. Winded, trying to regain your composure, raising your head. Your brain struggles to comprehend what you're looking at. An empty room. Danny, his clothes, everything, gone.

A chasm opens as you relive every harsh word and rejection from your father. A moan fills the room.

Reflection: Abandonment

"When one is abandoned, one is left alone. This can happen through physical absence as well as physical presence. In fact, to be abandoned by someone who is physically present is much more crazy-making."
— John Bradshaw

In childhood, we rely on others to support our feelings. When they don't — or are emotionally absent — we experience abandonment. It leads to fear of intimacy, lack of trust, anxiety, feelings of worthlessness and an overwhelming sense of being alone in this world. The fear of abandonment carries through to adult relationships — primarily romantic ones. Abandonment, like all inner child trauma, impacts us in many ways. But it is different for all of us. Here are some responses to an abandonment wound:

- *Constant worry that no one cares about us.*
- *Always looking for signs of rejection in our relationships.*
- *Trying to be perfect to avoid rejection.*
- *Becoming too attached to others for emotional security.*
- *Pushing people away to avoid being hurt.*
- *Ending relationships, fearing they will abandon us.*
- *Disconnecting from our feelings to avoid pain.*

At the core of our abandonment wound is a fear of being rejected. This leads to us ending our relationships before we're rejected, or we cling on so tightly that our lover leaves. We then question, 'Am I not good enough?' The fear of abandonment consumes every relationship we have. To heal, we must remind ourselves that we are worthy of love.

Adult Reaction: Sex Addiction

I remember being alone in Sydney and understanding that new places do not necessarily mean new freedoms. Our traumas continue to haunt us wherever we are.

My abandonment wound meant that when I got too close to someone, I'd pull away or find a reason to end the relationship. I wasn't able to engage in healthy, intimate relationships. I had affairs in an attempt to find love without intimacy. My focus was on sex.

The sex addiction began at an early age. I lost my virginity at the age of thirteen in Darwin's Botanical Gardens. But I believe the addiction started much earlier. At five, a girl invited me to a game of Spin the Bottle at her house. We ended up in a small cupboard under the stairs, and our lips met — of course, this was not about sex, but it triggered an addiction to the joy of having someone desire me. That moment of pleasure was an experience I wanted to repeat. More encounters followed to reinforce those feelings. On a ship from England to Australia, I went to a cabin with a girl to play doctor and patient. Once inside, she lay on the bunk, took off her swimmers and asked me to touch wherever she pointed. It added to my inner child's excitement and longing. Then, at eleven, I met a girl on holiday with my family. When they left me alone in the caravan, she joined me, and we kissed and touched each other. I used sex to cover up my pain and keep people at a distance. I wanted love but was fearful of it, so I engaged in shallow relationships and confused sex with love. Emotionally, I remained distant.

The desire to have someone care about us is vital for the wounded inner child. However, we must remember that our hurt happened long ago and that it takes time to heal. It's a journey of acknowledging the pain and engaging in self-care.

Healing Exercise: Embracing Vulnerability

To begin healing, we need to believe that we are valuable and can achieve love. It requires addressing past pain and building healthy relationships. We can do this through self-compassion and reparenting. Here are a series of steps that you can undertake to support your self-compassion journey:

1. *Recognise that the feelings of abandonment are real.*

2. *Understand that the pain came from the lack of emotional support, not because we are unworthy.*

3. *Give your inner child love and care.*

4. *Strengthen your inner self.*

5. Learn to say no and to put yourself first.

6. Seek relationships that are emotionally safe.

7. Challenge the thought that you are unlovable, replacing it with you are lovable.

Doing this work will strengthen your personal beliefs about yourself. It builds confidence and a sense of belonging. It is something we lost as children.

Consider cradling and comforting yourself in this next exercise. Start by holding a pillow against your chest as if holding your wounded inner child. Walk around, feeling the weight of your emotions. Let the tears flow. Release any pent-up feelings. Feel the feelings. As you continue to hold it close, reassure it that this release is safe and that healing is possible. This work is not a sign of weakness but one of strength — a commitment to growth.

Our early childhood wounds try to convince us that we're alone and trust is impossible. But in reality, we're not alone. We can have fulfilling, healthy relationships, starting with the one we build within ourselves. In the next chapter, we'll explore what happens when a surprise encounter leads me to believe that the worst is behind me, only to face a dramatic twist. My complex, unresolved traumas come to the fore again and shape how I react in this moment of crisis.

Chapter Ten

Echoes of Childhood

An old man, face pale, seated in the far corner of the cafe, coughs. A brown cardigan wrapped around his chest like a bandage. With a trembling hand, he picks up his cup. The contents slosh over the lip and into the saucer. With effort, he gets the cup to his lips; the slurp carries to you. The only other person in the cafe is the buxom lady behind the counter. As you ordered toast with a Coke, her *humph* suggested it is not an ideal breakfast.

Butter drips from the burnt toast. Shoving the plate away, turning to stare out of the window at the passing parade on Pitt Street.

The wind forcing many to hunker down in their coats, umbrellas appear as the rain starts.

With a sigh, turning back, you catch a glimpse of a boy bouncing down the People's Palace stairs. In contrast to his surroundings, on his head is a red top hat. Blonde hair peeks out from beneath the brim. He strides across the foyer as if the world is his.

The Bun, as you think of her now, watches closely.

I wanna meet him. You glance through the window to see which direction he went, but he's disappeared.

Hastening outside, not sure what you'll say if you do catch up with him, but knowing you must try. A flash of red makes your heart soar, racing towards it.

Coming to a sudden halt as an elderly lady turns around and, with a cold stare, wraps a red scarf tighter around her head. Apologising, you move on.

He can't just disappear. You run to Goulburn Street; nothing. Then to Castlereagh Street; still no sign of him.

The initial excitement fades as you crouch in a doorway, sheltering from the wind and rain. *There must be a way to find him. Maybe get his room number?* With a shake of your head. *No. The Bun won't help.*

Advertising signs bang and creak as the wind picks up. Bracing yourself, ready to step into the wind, spotting a handwritten note taped to the window where you're sheltering: Three-course meal for five dollars. Between six and eight.

Shit that's good. Got to remember this place.

The idea of sitting in your room doesn't appeal; memories of last night haunt you. Instead, you head to the television room.

A sagging yellow lounge in one corner. It looks preferable to the black vinyl chairs, flopping down, glad the room is bigger than yours.

To your surprise, the boy in the red top hat strides in. He halts and removes his hat.

A smile crosses your face. 'Great hat.'

He grins. 'Yeah. I bought it at the Cross. I'm Kevin.' He sits next to you.

Words tumble from you in an unstoppable flow, as if you've been friends forever. You tell him about Darwin, the trip, and, with a tremor in your voice, Danny leaving.

'That's shit. What'll you do?'

Shrugging, you don't reply. *What will I do?* Looking out the window, blue sky appears through the clouds; the rain has stopped.

A man steps into the room and shuffles past, a tattered raincoat over his shoulder. With a grunt, he takes a seat in a vinyl chair, drumming his fingers on one arm. His skin is the colour of dried porridge. He glances across, eyes stopping on you and then resting on Kevin.

Ignoring him, you turn back to Kevin. 'I found a place where for five bucks you get a three-course meal. I'm gonna go tonight. You wanna come?'

Kevin nods. 'Yeah. That sounds good.'

'There's plenty of those joints.' The man says, his voice like razor blades on metal. He sucks in air, snuffles, then continues, 'If you need a quid, I might be able to help youse.'

Squinting at him, not sure you heard correctly.

A blank expression on his face. 'There's a place over the road.' Lifting his chin, indicating the other side of the road. 'They got a window that's open. You know a person...', looking at you, 'Mebee your size could squeeze through. Might be a few quid in there for youse.'

Kevin mutters, 'No way.'

The man gets up, stopping at the door, he pulls the raincoat tighter around his shoulders. Looking back, his eyes slide over you. 'Let me know if youse get hungry.' With a snort, he leaves.

***

The five dollars buys three slices of roast beef, roast potatoes and pumpkin with two slices of buttered bread – a cup of tea and ice cream. Kevin, mouth full of meat and gravy, mumbles, 'Eat up. Never...' He burps. 'Never know where the next meal is going to come from.' Stuffing more food into his mouth, as if he's running late for an appointment. 'You decided what you'll do?'

You have, but it sounds stupid every time you run it around in your head. Exhaling, 'I wanna stay in Sydney. There's nothing for me in... in Darwin. But...'

You hesitate, remembering Craig's pleading eyes and the promise you made. 'I have a friend, umm, in Gambier. I was going with Danny, but now that he's...' Your voice trails away.

'That's a long way. You're not gonna hitch, are you?'

'No. I'll catch the bus. I haven't got a lot of money, but it shouldn't be too much.'

Kevin shrugs. 'When are you going?'

'Tomorrow. I'll look for a job when I get back.' You stare into the distance, knowing it sounds fanciful.

Kevin wipes his lips, slurps the last of his tea. Putting the cup down. 'C'mon, let me show you around. Could go to the snooker place. Gotta be careful though, it's a Sharpie hangout.'

'Sharpie? What's a Sharpie?'

He grins, looking at you as if you're from another world. 'Shit, where've you been?'

You wait for him to continue.

'Sharpies think they own the streets.' He paused. 'I guess they do. They wear metal-capped boots and roam around in gangs, and like to kick the shit out of anyone they don't like.' He laughs, picking at his nose, inspecting the findings and flicking it on the floor. 'That's you and me, 'coz they hate long hair. That's what they call us, long hairs,' he says, smiling. 'Anyway, run if you see 'em.'

Reaching George Street, Kevin tugs on your sleeve, struggling to breathe.

Concerned with how he looks, you put an arm around his shoulders. 'You okay?'

His breathing slows, and he nods. 'I got asthma. It's a pain.' His face is ghostly white. The snooker room forgotten, he clutches your arm as you help him back to the Palace.

On the steps, you hesitate – the Bun's in the booth. You take Kevin aside so she can't see.

'What will you do when I go see my friend?'

Kevin's brow furrows, then, in a low voice, 'Go visit me mum.' He stares across the street.

You grip his arm. 'You'll come back? Won't you? I don't, I haven't got...'

Kevin smiles. 'Shit yeah. I'm gonna help you find a job.' He leans closer. 'Take your stuff. They'll let you leave it, but they'll charge you.'

Nodding, wishing now you weren't going. You want to hug him, but showing affection is not something you're used to or even know how to do. The thought makes you withdraw.

Why can't I? You punch him lightly on the arm, promising to be back in a few days.

Striding past the Bun and up the stairs, her eyes never leaving you. You couldn't have known what was about to happen. If you had, maybe you would have stayed.

***

Wearily making your way back to the People's Palace, the bag weighing heavily on your shoulder. The two tickets in your pocket are a reminder of the man on the bus.

He'd begged for five dollars, offering them in exchange. As you handed him the money, he embraced you. It was both warm and frightening. The tickets were for something called *Hair*. *Maybe I can sell them?* Halting on the steps of the Palace, your head drops. *Doesn't she ever go home?*

The Bun rolls her eyes. 'You're back?'

'Yes, can I...'

She interrupts. 'The Major wants to speak with you.'

'The Major? Who... me? Why? Can I, why?'

'He said if you came back, you had to see him before you were allowed to have a room. That's why.'

'Tomorrow, I'm...'

Slamming her hand down on the counter, 'If you want a room, you'll speak with him now.' She nods towards a door, *OFFICE* in gold lettering on it.

Beads of sweat break out on your forehead as you approach. Looking over your shoulder, you see a glint of satisfaction in her eyes.

She knows what's gonna happen.

You knock.

A voice like a breeze through grass whispers, 'Come in.' A thin-faced man, a pair of rimless glasses perched on the end of his cherry-coloured nose, studies you as you enter. He nods towards a chair in front of his desk. You oblige, trying to figure out what's happening.

He stands, slips off his dark-blue jacket and hangs it on a coat rack near a timber bookshelf. A single book on the shelves. He sits, fiddles with a peaked cap resting on a pile of papers, eventually glancing at you.

Why isn't he saying anything?

Tensing, you wait.

Removing his glasses, he pulls out a handkerchief and polishes them, placing them back on his nose. The silence continues. Then: 'I'm Major Freck.'

You open your mouth. 'Uh, umm, the lady, she...' You point back towards the door. 'She said you wanted to talk to me, if I...?'

'Yes. Quite, quite,' he muttered. 'I'm concerned about... about a friend of yours. Let me...' He removes the cap from the pile of papers. Shuffling through them, picking one up, squinting at it over his glasses. 'Ah yes, Kevin Watts, that's his name. He's your friend?'

Why is he asking about Kevin? Is it the same Kevin? 'Um, I don't know his surname.'

The sheet of paper goes back down on his desk. Removing the glasses, rubbing his eyes, he stares at you. 'He's the boy who wears that silly hat, correct?'

'Oh, yes. He's my friend.'

Shaking his head, 'Your friend has caused trouble for one of our elderly residents.'

You hesitate, not completely surprised. 'He wouldn't.' A lump in the pit of your stomach as you wait.

Shit, what's Kevin done?

The Major continued. 'This says he entered the room of an elderly woman. Do you know anything about that?'

'It's a lie.'

His voice hardened. 'My staff don't lie, and I am sure the resident doesn't. We called the police and your friend disappeared. That's not the action of an innocent person, is it? I'll not tolerate any behaviour that upsets our guests.'

'I wasn't here. I didn't do anything.'

Pinching his nose with a forefinger and thumb, sighing, 'I know you weren't here, and that's the only reason I'm letting you stay. But, and I mean this, young man, any trouble and I'll not hesitate to ask you to leave. Do you understand?'

Relieved, you nod.

'Make sure you do. Good night.'

Could he have done it?

The Bun's eyes are scathing as you stand in front of her for a second time.

'Can I get a room, please?'

She sneers. 'So, he's letting you stay. You should be out on the street.'

'Can I have a room for, umm, five nights please?'

'That's one hundred and twenty-five dollars.'

Your mouth drops open. 'Uh, that's, that's more than last time.'

'Yes. Prices go up. Other people want these rooms.'

'Um. I can't.' Shaking your head. 'I haven't got that much.'

Sniggering, 'Then go across the street. It's better suited to your type anyway. Now, I'm busy.'

Your shoulders slump, beaten. 'Um, four nights? Please?'

'What? Speak up.'

'Four nights.'

Glaring, her mouth opens to say something, but thinking better of it, she closes it again. 'That's one hundred. You got that?'

As you reach to take the key from her fingers, she holds onto it.

'I'm watching you. Any trouble, and you'll be out.'

The room is the same as the other, apart from a bedside table and clock radio. Hurling your bag into a corner, emptying your pockets onto the bed, dismayed at what's left.

Two worthless tickets and sixty cents. There must be an explanation. Shit, how will I find Kevin? You look at the pathetic amount of money on the bed.

Maybe take up the stranger's offer?

Shaking your head. *No. Kevin mentioned catching a train to go home, but where's the station?*

Sleep eludes you, as you are racked with fear and guilt for leaving him; heart thumping, feeling sick in the stomach.

Why does stuff like this keep happening? How can I trust anyone?

Reflection: Complex Trauma

"Our problem is not that as children our needs were unmet, but that as adults they are still unmourned." — David Richo

Complex trauma develops through prolonged exposure to trauma over a period of time. As our trauma occurred in childhood, we had no understanding of why it was happening, so we concluded that it was our fault. The trauma is so deep that a fragment of a memory, a smell or sound can trigger a huge emotional reaction. That reaction is usually anger and rage. Abused children spend their childhood learning to survive in an abusive environment. We live on the edge, constantly scanning for danger and ready to react. It's exhausting. Many adults who suffered childhood abuse talk about continually feeling tired. There are common reactions to complex trauma. They include:

- *Difficulty controlling emotions or anger.*
- *Feeling guilty and shameful even when there's no reason to.*
- *Unable to maintain healthy relationships.*
- *Become involved in abusive relationships, replicating your childhood abuse.*
- *Have difficulty trusting people.*
- *Become addicted to alcohol, drugs, pornography or sex.*
- *Feel that you don't belong in this world.*
- *Have thoughts of suicide.*

With this much trauma in our bodies, you might ask how we function as healthy adults. The answer is that many of us don't. The rest act fine, but in reality, we're a churning mass of trauma that can erupt at any time.

Complex trauma also causes the physiological symptoms of adrenal exhaustion or fatigue. Although not a medical diagnosis, adrenal fatigue occurs because the adrenal glands can't keep up with the constant demand of our fight-or-flight state. Because we are continually vigilant for danger, we experience tiredness, weakness and difficulty sleeping. Talk to a trauma victim, and they'll tell you of the fatigue they experience every day. Even when not in a trauma-inducing situation. If triggered, trauma sufferers feel exhausted, ashamed and sad following a traumatic response. I understand that we can have those symptoms for many reasons, and complex trauma should be considered as one of the reasons, too.

Post-Traumatic Stress Disorder (PTSD) and Complex Post-Traumatic Stress Disorder (CPTSD) are sometimes considered the same. However, although similar, there are differences. PTSD develops from a singular event, such as being in an armed conflict, violent altercation or being involved in an emergency. The individual is under stress for an extended period and, during that time, develops PTSD. An example of this would be the attack on the World Trade Centre. Many first responders were diagnosed with PTSD. The trauma responses to PTSD are flashbacks, nightmares, hypervigilance, avoiding trauma reminders and emotional numbing. CPTSD is different in that it is the ongoing emotional wounding of a child. Its symptoms are shame, guilt, anger, rejection, injustice, abandonment and betrayal. However, both PTSD and CPTSD can be treated and healed in similar ways.

Adult Reaction: Rage

As adults, we can suffer from simultaneous traumas due to complex trauma. Kevin's disappearance sent me into a downward spiral that I hadn't experienced before. It was as if my fear, abandonment, anger and grief all combined to weigh me down.

My rage can be triggered by noise. It has become a significant issue for me, particularly in my efforts to control it. Of course, in a world filled with noise, this is impossible. A loud or sudden noise causes my inner child to shrink in fear and react with anger and rage. When it takes over, my reasoning disappears.

The reason noise triggers my complex trauma is that I grew up in a home where my parents settled their differences by screaming at each other. Even when they weren't fighting, I would walk on eggshells, waiting for their next outburst. I don't remember when they were not at each other's throats. I couldn't escape and was powerless to stop the noise. So, I lived in fear. My nervous system absorbed that fear; now, sudden noise brings back those repressed memories, and I relive my childhood fear.

My mother had her own unresolved trauma and was also prone to violent outbursts. One day, her rage got out of control – she threw a knife at me for playing with my food. It struck my head, drawing blood. She rushed me to the hospital in my sister's baby carriage.

All of this created a trauma that left me associating noise with violence. I also assume I would've experienced their screaming from birth. These memories are termed as implicit. They happen before we have a voice, so we can't put words to the trauma. Even though we can't recall them, implicit memory still has an impact and makes us hyper-vigilant and afraid. We don't understand these reactions because we have no words to describe the trauma as it occurred before we could speak. This contributes to a feeling of impending doom, even when safe.

Healing Exercise: Calming Therapy

Complex trauma requires a holistic approach to healing. Therapies like somatic breathing, attachment-focused treatment, and emotional reprocessing will assist in the process. All of these will empower you. Undertaking meditation and yoga will also help, as will joining a support group. Both PTSD and CPTSD sufferers can find relief with these therapies.

This somatic breathing exercise will provide calm for your nervous system when you are stressed. Somatic breathwork can also have a physical response, such as shaking or trembling. As always, the more we repeat these exercises, the more benefit we gain.

1. *Begin by sitting or lying down.*

2. *Breathe in and hold your breath and count to ten.*

3. *When you reach ten, breathe out and sigh. This helps release all of your breath.*

4. *Now, breathe in through your nose for three seconds and out for three seconds.*

5. *This will produce a breathing rate of ten breaths per minute.*

6. *Hold your breath for ten seconds after every ten breaths.*

7. *Continue breathing through your nose for three seconds and out for three seconds.*

8. *Do this exercise until all feelings of anxiety are gone.*

Healing complex trauma may require help from a professional who specialises in inner child work. I also have resources to assist you on your healing journey.

In the next chapter, when confronted by authority, my reaction goes beyond the moment itself. This interaction triggers my authority wound, reminding me I'm powerless. How can I separate my trauma from reality and not feel helpless? Let's explore the impacts of the authority wound.

Chapter Eleven

Rebelling Against Control

Wiping her hands, face creasing into a smile, she doesn't appear to mind that you haven't bought anything. 'Which station, love? Town Hall or Central.'

Shrugging, not sure. You'd thought there was only one, and hoped Kevin would turn up and then everything would go back to the way it was.

'Central's closest dear. Turn left out of the cafe and follow Pitt Street. You can't miss it.'

***

The fear that you won't see Kevin again is a solid lump in your belly. Pushing the thought aside, you stare one by one at everyone alighting from the arriving trains.

This is my only hope.

An old woman staggers in your direction. Her gaze fixed on the bench. You hope she'll pass by, but instead sits, arranging her woollen coat over her knees. Tufts of grey poke from beneath a greasy Levi cap. Snuffling and coughing, taking a quick glance at you before wiping her nose with the back of her hand. Mottled blue flesh shows through black stockings; a red sand shoe on one foot, white on the other. Pulling out a newspaper, she spreads it across the bench as if she's in a library.

Looking away, you're only interested in the arrival of the next train, hoping the lady in the cafe is correct, that this is the best station to try. A rattling sound signifies another train is arriving.

Will he be on this one?

The old lady sniffs and stands, putting on her coat, throwing a haughty look at you as she leaves. Watching her walk away, amused at the cap sitting at an angle on her head, giving her a youthful appearance. You sense she may have been a lady of means at one stage. She left the paper.

How much longer should I wait? A breeze ruffles the newspaper. Shrugging — *Why not?* You pick it up. *You never know, there might be a job.*

Flicking through, you see jobs for bricklayers and factory workers, in places you've never heard of. Screwing the paper up in disgust, you're about to chuck it away when your eye catches a headline: 'Dishwasher wanted for leading city restaurant.' Your heart skips a beat.

City restaurant. Smoothing the page, you read further. Interviews at three on Tuesday at Albert's Restaurant, Double Bay.

Shit, that's today. Where is Double Bay? The railway clock shows one. You might make it.

Gotta find the train to Double Bay.

Thirty minutes later, you throw your hands up in the air. There's no Double Bay on any of the train boards.

How do I get there?

Rushing to a ticket booth, fingers crossed, 'Uh, can you tell me...?'

Without looking up, the man in the booth snaps, 'Where to?'

'Double Bay.'

He exhales, looking up. 'Are you joking, son? Trains don't go to Double Bay.'

With a frustrated shake of your head, 'Oh. Uh, how can, how do I get there?'

'Catch a bus. You'll find 'em out front. Next.'

You remember seeing buses lined up at the entrance to the station. Ten minutes later there's still no sign of a bus that goes to Double Bay. Time is ticking.

I mustn't be late.

You approach a man dispensing tickets. 'Ticket to Double Bay, please?'

No buses to Double Bay from here, son.'

'Where do I get one?'

He pauses, scanning your appearance. 'Double Bay's a bit posh. Sure, you got the right place?'

'I... um, yes. I'm going for a job.'

He laughs. 'A job? Sure.' With a cold laugh, 'You have a job in Double Bay. Okay, I believe you. Thousands wouldn't. Go up Pitt Street.' Pointing back the way you'd come. 'To Park Street, near Hyde Park. Do you know where that is?' Nodding. Kevin and you had walked through Hyde Park that first night. The thought makes your stomach rumble. Shaking it off as he continues, 'You'll find buses leaving for Double Bay from there.'

Thinking of the meagre sixty cents in your pocket, 'Uh, how much to get there?'

Tapping his fingers on the ticket machine, he sighs. 'Not sure son, probably fifty cents.'

Nodding a thanks, relieved you have enough, but you've lost track of the time. *Must hurry.*

Dashing across Belmore Park, you don't notice the white sedan parked in the middle, four men inside.

***

Hesitating at the entrance to Albert's Restaurant, your enthusiasm long gone. You know how you must look — tattered clothes, hot and sweaty.

Is it worth going in?

There's no other choice, Kevin's return is a pipe dream, even if it's one you're not yet ready to let go of. *No, not yet.*

You enter.

The front bar is dominated by an archway. You see tables draped in white cloth with red velvet chairs around them. Feeling out of place, turning to leave, a man behind an oak bar polishing a glass pauses. 'Can I help you?' His voice is high-pitched.

Throat dry, you turn back and face him. 'Uh, I came about, about the job.'

'What?'

'The dishwashing job.'

'Oh. That. I'm afraid I've already offered it to someone.'

'Oh.'

'You, okay? Do you need to sit down? You look like you might collapse.'

'I'm... I'm fine.' Hiding your disappointment, you reach for the door handle.

The man puts the glass down. 'Hang on. Wait, wait a minute. Do you need the job that badly?'

'Umm, I need a job. That's all.' Tears prick the corners of your eyes. You need to get away.

'How long have you been looking?'

Wanting to run out the door, instead muttering, 'I've just started.'

'You sure you're alright?'

'Yes. I'm fine.'

'When was your last meal? I mean a decent one.'

'Uh...' barely able to refrain from licking your lips. 'I'm okay, really.'

His eyes soften. 'Look, I can't do anything about the job. But I can offer you a meal. So come and sit down.'

'I do... I don't know, I don't have money.'

'It's on me,' throwing the cloth on the bar, glancing in the mirror, straightening his bow tie. 'Have a seat. I'm Richard, I manage this place.' A smirk on his face. 'We're closed, but the chef's still here. I'll get him to cook you a steak. How's that?'

Sitting in the velvet chair, running your hands over the crisp white tablecloth, feeling out of place as Richard returns.

'It won't be long. Let me make you one of my favourite drinks. That'll cheer you up.' He reappears with a glass of clear liquid, a slice of lemon floating on top. With a smile, 'It's a gin and tonic. I'll be in the bar if you need anything.' As he turns to leave, he stops and inspects the back of a chair, then flicks a piece of fluff off and sniffs.

Your nose wrinkles at the bitter taste of the drink. Over the rim of the glass, you watch a lady stroll towards you, steam rising from the plate in her hands.

'Hello. I see you've got Richard's favourite drink. He does like his gin and tonics.'

Embarrassed, smiling shyly, 'I don't think I do.'

She laughs, a sweet sound. 'It's an acquired taste, a bit like Richard. So, what's your story?'

There is a comfortable warmth in her manner, or maybe it's the gin and tonic.

You tell her about the trip, including Danny and the money, leaving out the part about Kevin. 'I came for the dishwasher job, but it's gone. He offered me a meal. It's nice of him.'

She winks. 'It is. Enjoy.'

Swallowing the last of the gin and tonic, you sit back with a satisfied smile on your face and a full stomach.

The lady returns. 'I take it you liked that?' You can't stop grinning as she picks up the plate, replacing it with a twenty-dollar note. 'This is for you. Take care.'

'Uh, oh, I can't pay you back.'

'No need. I know what it's like to be broke.'

Richard holds onto your hand as he says goodbye, 'Come back if you need help, and I'll see what I can do.'

Settling into your seat on the bus, smiling to yourself. You don't need Richard's help. Everything's going to be alright.

***

The past three hours at the station have given you nothing but a cold bum and stiff back. A voice inside insists that Kevin's not coming back, ever. Once again, you consider the offer by the man in the television room. The idea of talking to him on your own scares you, let alone doing what he suggests.

What if it's the only way?

With a bowed head, you decide to head back to the Palace, admitting defeat.

A white car is in the middle of the park; a niggle in the back of your mind; ignoring it, you plod on — you've decided to wait in the television room and see if he turns up.

The weight in your chest suggests he will.

The sun disappears behind clouds. Shivering, wishing you'd worn your vest.

Two nights left. What's next? Suddenly, the white car is blocking your way.

What's it doing there? Stomach churning, you drop your gaze, praying this is not going to be trouble.

The doors open and four men, the size of front-row forwards, get out. Moving as one, eight hard, unblinking eyes stare at you. A finger, fat as a pork sausage, points. 'Your name, is it Robinson?'

How does he know my name? You nod, shifting from foot to foot.

What do they want? Another step closer, back-pedalling as he flashes a card in your face. 'We're police officers and we want to talk to you. You're staying at the People's Palace, is that correct?'

Trembling, their expressions shatter all thoughts of talking to the man in the television room, and of looking for Kevin.

'We're looking for a friend of yours.' Snaps the man with the card.

'I..., who...'

Interrupting, he points towards the railway station. 'What were you doing in there? Waiting for a train?'

An ice-cold laugh followed.

Shoving your hands into your pockets so they can't see them shaking, 'I. Oh, I... I was... waiting for...'

Words fail you. *What can I say?*

'Waiting? Waiting for what?'

'Umm.'

'Is that all you have to say? Are you an idiot?'

Another sneers. 'We asked what the fuck you were doing in there? This friend assaulted an old lady. Did you enjoy watching him do it?'

The fourth one shouts, 'Say something you little shit.'

'He, he wouldn't.'

'Wouldn't, huh? Did you meet him there?' Nodding towards the station, 'Maybe gloat over what you did?' His hand smacks the car bonnet, startling you. Unable to look at him, you stare at the ground. 'Well, did you? Are you planning something else?'

Could they know about the other man? Voice shaking, 'No. I. He. I didn't.'

The man closest to you grabs your arm, and squeezes. 'You're coming with us.'

Struggling to free yourself. 'Why? Where?'

His grip tightens. 'Because we say so.' His breath reeks of onions.

You try to wrench out of his grip. 'I didn't do anything. I don't know where Kevin is. He's gone.' Fighting back tears.

'We want to have a look at your room. Now get in the car.'

People hurry past, averting their eyes, not wanting to get involved with another youth causing trouble.

The officer leads you to the rear of the car and sits on one side while another slides in on the other side. The smell of stale hamburger, cigarette smoke and sweat fill the vehicle along with fear. A police radio crackles. Grunting, the man behind the wheel leans over and switches it off.

'How long have you known this, Kevin?' the largest of the men asks, his stomach wobbling each time the car hits a bump.

'I... um, a few days.'

'You meet him at the People's Palace?' You nod. 'Were you with him when he assaulted the old lady?'

'No. He wouldn't hurt anyone. He's not like that.'

'Is that right? You know that after a few days, do you?' A ghoulish imitation of a grin on his face. 'I bet you both enjoyed it.'

The car comes to a halt in the middle of Pitt Street, opposite the Palace. The two men on either side get out, one leans back in, his face inches from yours, 'Get out. I want to see your room. Now!'

'I haven't done anything.'

Grabbing your shirt collar, he drags you out of the car.

With a hand on the back of your neck, he steers you across the road and up the steps.

The Bun, in her usual place, has a malicious grin on her face. She watches as you're frog-marched across the foyer, her grin growing ever wider. A quick exchange of nods between her and one of the men confirms your suspicions.

She told them. The bitch.

The man with his hand around your neck snaps, 'Show us your room.' Leading the way, heart racing.

What'll happen once they're inside my room?

Stopping at the door, the man with his hand on your neck squeezes, then lets go, as you search for the key. 'Give it here,' he demands.

A guest in a bathrobe, hair dripping, shuffles past, turning his head away as your door is unlocked and you're pushed inside. 'How long have you been here?'

'A few nights. I'm moving out as soon as I find a job.'

'No job?' Your heart stops.

Shit, keep your mouth shut.

Picking your bag up, tipping the contents onto the bed, they paw through it. The cowboy vest is hanging over the end of the bed, and one picks it up, examining it. 'Did you steal this?' The *Hair* tickets fall to the floor. 'What are these?' Picking them up, he swipes you across the face with them. 'Where did you get them?'

'I, uh, someone gave them to me.'

'Who'd give you these? I bet a bob to nothing that you stole them.' He tucks them away. 'I'll keep em,' patting his pocket.

The other officer lets out a long slow whistle. 'Well, well, well. What do we have here?' He's holding your bowie knife. Your stomach drops to your toes.

Shit. Shit. You'd forgotten all about it.

'Is this yours?' Gulping, you nod. 'Why do you have a knife?'

'To... to protect me.'

He lets out a snort. 'From what, old ladies?' Sliding it out of its sheaf, it catches the light, shining wickedly in his hand. 'Have you used it?' Your legs wobble.

Does this mean I'm going to jail?

The largest officer growls, 'You're lucky kid. The manager confirmed you weren't here when the lady was assaulted. But this is a warning. Stay out of trouble and away from this Kevin character ... or else.' He tucked the cowboy vest under his arm. 'I'll keep this.'

'And we'll keep this,' says the one holding the knife, putting it under his jacket. 'Can't have you wandering around the city with it.'

Stopping at the door, the large one turns back. 'It would be best if you crawled back under the rock you came from. If we see you again…' The door closes with a thud.

You curl up on your bed, screaming into the pillow.

***

Her footsteps echo across the lobby as she pounds towards you, arms swinging, blue dress billowing like a tent in a windstorm.

If I can make it to the stairs, I'll be okay.

She blocks the way, legs planted, chest heaving. Gasping, 'The Major…' A wheeze, 'Wants…' Another gasp. You hope she collapses, pitying the floor. 'Wants… wants… see you.' Florid cheeks puff as she exhales.

'Can I see him tomorrow?'

Regaining her breath, she pulls herself up to her full height, five feet in your estimation. 'No. He said when you came back!'

You look towards the office door, then at the stairs. She's won. 'You wanted to see me?'

The Major looks up from his newspaper, then places it on the desk. Thin fingers cup his chin as his watery eyes roam up and down your face.

The hair on the back of your neck stands on end, waiting for him to speak. His whispering voice carries clearly to you. 'The police. What did they want?'

She must've told him. 'Umm, nothing. Wanted to see my room, that's all.'

'Why?'

A shrug. 'I don't know.'

'Police don't inspect a person's room for no reason.'

'They asked about Kevin.'

'Do you remember what I said last time?' He didn't wait for a reply. 'I told you I didn't want any trouble. Police dragging a resident through our lobby is the sort of thing I was talking about.'

'They didn't...'

Interrupting, 'This Kevin.' He spat the name out as if it left a nasty taste in his mouth. 'He's caused enough trouble already. I don't want any more. I want you to leave in the morning.'

'I didn't do anything.' The whine in your voice pisses you off. 'I've got two nights left. I'll go after that. Please. I've got nowhere to go.'

His lips press together. 'Beth will refund one night. Consider yourself lucky. She recommended we put you out tonight.'

Sniffing, you mutter, 'I bet. This isn't fair.'

Picking up his paper, flicking it open, dismissing you.

The Bun has an unpleasant smile on her face as you rush past and up the stairs to your room.

All I've got is ten dollars. Where can I go? Who can I ask for help?

Slumping onto the bed, memories of a Valiant, a coconut tree, an emergency room, Alan and Danny swirl in your head. A tremor grips you as your thoughts reel to the Vic Hotel. With a sob.

Why's everything so difficult?

***

Waking with a start, your arm wrapped around the pillow. Legs dangling over the end of the bed, the soles of your feet encrusted with dirt. One big toe throbs.

What happened?

A vague memory of creeping along a hallway, stumbling over an empty bucket, kicking it with your foot, sending it rattling across the floor. Squeaking bed springs and a grumbling female voice.

Who would leave a bucket in a hallway?

A rooftop floats into your vision, the wind howling and driving rain against your cheek. Your flannelette shirt, no match. You wish you had your buckskin vest.

The bastards.

A metal door bangs, looking over your shoulder, fearing someone else is with you. No-one. It won't matter soon. The city lights twinkle, reminding you of Christmas and your father yelling at the tree lights when they wouldn't work. Your nose wrinkles at the stink of garbage and car fumes floating up from the street.

Whoever said rain washes a city clean is wrong. It makes human stench worse.

Taking the slip of paper out of your pocket, turning it over and over in your hands, knowing no one would care even if they got to read it.

Fuck 'em. With shaking hands, you tear it into strips, throwing them in the air. The wind carries them away over the city skyline. The door bangs again but this time you ignore it. Something more pressing is on your mind.

Your cheeks are damp, even though the rain has stopped.

With a dejected sigh, you edge towards the end of the roof. Your body weighing you down... you begin to tremble uncontrollably. Collapsing to the ground as a greater fear grips you.

Shaking your head, the images fade. You're still unsure about what you saw or what happened. A scrap of paper is stuck to your jeans.

Sniffling, you know you have to leave, but where will you go? Richard's words: *Come back if you need help, and I'll see what I can do.* You know he'll help, but... You felt a tension in him. *Tension is wrong. Secrets, that's it, his secrets.*

The lady said he was an acquired taste. *What does that mean?*

The idea of accepting the offer from the man in the television room makes you tremble. Suddenly, your mind fills with the image of two imposing police officers, blocking out all other thoughts.

I can't.

***

The Bun isn't in the booth, which brings a smile to your lips and a sigh of relief — until you spy an even larger woman in there, with a face that appears to be set in stone. She surveys the lobby as if it's her domain, and only hers. A canary-yellow dress is fighting a losing battle to contain her breasts. They jiggle like mounds of jelly each time she moves. She shakes her head as you ask for your refund. 'We don't give refunds.'

'The Major said I'd get a refund.'

'Wait here.' She shuffles across the floor to the office. Knocking, she enters without invitation. Five minutes later, flustered, she's back. 'Sooo,' she puffs, squeezing back into the booth, 'The Major says you get a refund for one night. Consider yourself lucky.' She thrusts ten dollars towards you with a sniff. 'Take this and don't come back. We don't want the likes of you in here.'

Opening your mouth to argue that it should be twenty-five dollars, but one look at her makes you decide otherwise.

The offer from the man in the television room fades to nothing.

It has to be Richard. The realisation clenches your chest, your breathing shallow as you slink away.

Reflection: Authority Wound

"Man's main task is to give birth to himself, to become what he potentially is."
— Erich Fromm

The authority wound is about loss of self-worth and autonomy. As children, we quickly understand what our caregivers need and our role within the home. We attempt to please them to protect ourselves. When we realise they want us to be submissive, we oblige — giving up our original selves in the process. If they use excessive discipline, ridicule us in front of others or ignore us when we need comfort, we associate these responses with feeling powerless. Over time, this leads to us becoming nervous, anxious, or submissive in the presence of authority. We ignore our own needs in favour of others. We find ourselves unable to ask others for help, believing we must do everything ourselves. We feel we are selfish if we want something for ourselves and suppress our opinions to avoid conflict. For many of us, it will manifest as a fear of responsibility or leadership. It's not that we are incapable of responsibility or leadership. It's that we believe we are not worthy.

When we take the authority wound into our relationships, we struggle to assert ourselves, dreading the possibility of rejection or ridicule. Due to this, we try to claim our self-worth by confrontation, as the years of suppressed emotion make us defensive or angry.

Adult Reaction: Monster Within

My fear of authority was displayed whenever I was challenged or had to deal with authority. When confronted by the police officers in Sydney, I froze with fear and anxiety. I imagined the worst, even though I'd done nothing wrong. The same occurred when I had to leave the People's Palace. Again, I was innocent of wrongdoing but was too afraid to speak up or defend myself. When I tried, my internal voice would shut me down as the authority wound took away my self-belief. My most significant challenge has been overcoming my aggressive responses when challenged. Such reactions have hindered my career and ability to make close friends. It has led to a feeling of insecurity and anxiety. My authority wound surfaced whenever I was in a position of leadership. I would turn into a monster. I became angry over minor issues. As shown in the chapter on bullying, our emotional overreactions are not limited to one singular trauma. My threats of physical violence towards colleagues also surfaced when I felt my authority was challenged. When pointed out to me, I was still not self-aware enough to challenge or question my reactions. I became the person I hated and feared as a child, my father. It led to me avoiding responsibility as I believed I was not capable of, or deserved responsibility.

The authority wound dramatically impacts our adult lives, from personal to professional. See if any of the following authority wound responses resonate with you.

- *Resisting rules or rejecting leadership by others.*

- *Reacting negatively to feedback or control.*

- *Unable to say no, even in unfair or harmful situations.*

- *Avoiding decision-making due to fear of rejection.*

- *Believing you're incapable of being in charge.*

- *Needing constant approval from bosses or friends to feel worthy.*

- *Feeling lost or anxious without external help.*

- *Allowing people in authority to overstep their limits.*

- *Feeling obliged to follow the rules, even when unreasonable.*

- *Feeling like a fraud in leadership positions.*

- *Questioning your worthiness for success.*

- *Becoming controlling or submissive in personal relationships.*

- *Struggling with trust in relationships.*

If you recognise any of these in yourself, know that they are all symptoms of the authority wound resulting from childhood abuse — these, more often than not, surface as a complicated mix of emotional reactions. The good news is that we can heal the authority wound once we understand what motivates our emotional responses.

Healing Exercise: Becoming You

Healing begins with recognising the response of the authority wound and challenging the idea that we are unworthy. We must tell ourselves we are important and we matter. Start by implementing some simple decision-making steps. It could be arranging an event at a workplace or ordering business supplies. Take ownership of your capabilities and decisions. Treat yourself gently, and don't rush; take one step at a time. Also, if asked to do something that you don't want to do, politely decline and don't be persuaded otherwise.

A common theme in our healing is the need to rediscover play. We need to nurture and provide simple joy to our inner child. I remember the happiness I felt when my father would take the time to sit and play a board game. It was rare and was followed by sadness when he left. But play is something we can reclaim. It'll help us find the childlike feelings we lost. Join a community that plays cards or board games. There are also online groups you can connect with, or others struggling with similar issues. This will give you a sense of belonging and community. Find a sport that suits you. Make sure it's fun and not competitive. The inner child can get very competitive and be a sore loser.

Our friends may change as we build a new us, and family members will look at us oddly. They don't understand who we are becoming. Remember, the real us has been hiding for a long time. Healing is about rebuilding a sense of identity and authority. Here's a practice that will help support you on this journey. Remember, repetition of this practice is vital for rebuilding a sense of worth. Begin by asking yourself: 'If I'd been loyal to myself, what would I have done differently?' It's a way to look inward and to build better intentions. Ask again: 'If I'd been loyal to myself, then what would I have done differently?' You might answer with, 'I would have taken the lead in a discussion,' or 'I would have said no when asked to do something I didn't want to do.' By changing our thought patterns, we start believing in ourselves and quieting the negative thoughts. Remember that integrity and authenticity are essential when reawakening our true selves.

Authority and guilt are closely intertwined. The guilt of being an unloved child drove me to say yes when I meant no. My guilt also led me to accept an offer I knew could have consequences — not because I wanted to but because I had to. The guilt wound is one of submission. But the consequences can be catastrophic when linked to the authority wound. Guilt often drives our decisions as adults. Let's explore guilt and ways to heal in the next chapter.

Chapter Twelve

Burden of Blame

Richard stood in the same spot as he had last time. Then, you were desperate for a job. Now, you're desperate for a place to stay.

Will he help?

He was busy polishing glasses, his focus unwavering.

An unease settled over you. Stronger than before. It wasn't just discomfort this time. It felt like fear. Of what, you couldn't say.

'Well, look what the cat has dragged in. Back for another steak?' Richard sniggered, throwing a dish cloth in your direction, 'Here. Dry yourself. So, what brings you back to my little establishment?'

Teeth chattering, water pooling at your feet, 'I...' Stopping, embarrassed as a girl bounces into the room, coming to a halt as she glances at Richard and then at you.

'Everything okay, Richard?'

'Yep. This is a friend of mine.' He flicks his wrist at her in a dismissive manner. Sniffing, the girl leaves, slamming the door behind her. 'Sorry about that. You were saying?'

'Uh, you said you might help me. If I...' *this is stupid.* 'I understand if you can't. I'll go.'

'Wait. What happened?'

'I need ...' looking at your feet, 'I've got nowhere else to go.'

You glance up to see how this statement has been received. His eyes have a faraway, as if he's considering something.

You shouldn't have come. He won't help.

'My mum,' he finally says, 'God rest her soul, always said you should keep your word. I can put you up for a few nights.'

'Thank you. It's only until I find, I mean, meet my friend.'

'Alright. Let me finish here. Then we'll go.' Turning away, he picks up a glass, vigorously wiping it while humming to himself, then inspecting it, nodding, placing it on a shelf.

You're not sure what to do.

Has he forgotten about me?

There isn't anywhere to sit other than the velvet-covered chairs; you remain where you are as he continues to fuss with the glasses.

Wiping down the bar with a grand sweep, he stands back to admire his work. 'Okay, let's get out of here. The car's out back. Go through the kitchen.'

Hesitating, you glance towards the restaurant.

'It's okay. Everyone's gone.' He crosses over to you, placing an arm around your shoulders. Stiffening, he quickly drops his arm, looking at you from the corner of his eye. 'Go through there,' pointing to the kitchen door. 'I'll put on the alarm.'

You push open a steel door and step into a walled courtyard. The stench of rotting vegetables is overwhelming — *What a waste.*

Richard, close behind, takes hold of your arm. 'C'mon. It's this way.' He guides you across the courtyard to a blue car, the interior refreshing after the rotting vegetables. 'It's only the cat and me at home,' he says, pulling into the street. 'Hope you'll be comfortable.'

You concentrate on street names, knowing you'll need to find your way back to Central.

Can't give up on Kevin. Not yet.

'Here we are.' Opening the front door, he bows. 'Welcome to my humble abode.' A cat races down the hallway, its claws click on the timber floor, sliding to a halt against his leg. Bending down, you run a hand along its back. It purrs. Richard laughs. 'She likes you. C'mon, let me show you your bedroom.' He leads you down a hallway adorned with black and white photos of semi-naked men. Flinging a door open, to a room not much bigger than the one at the Palace. There's a set of bunk beds against the wall and nothing else, not even a rug. 'Here's your boudoir. I hope you find it comfortable. Take the top or bottom bunk.' He winks. 'I prefer the bottom.'

Missing the innuendo, 'The bottom's fine.'

His eyes linger on your face, and then, with a wave, 'Put your things down and I'll start dinner. Quick and easy tonight, like me.' As he goes to leave, 'Take a shower. You could do with one.'

Peeling off your clothes, tired to the bone, you drop them on the bathroom floor, making a dirty pile on the pristine white tiles.

I'll pick them up after the shower.

You've noticed Richard's fastidious ways and don't want to upset him. The hot water soaks into your pores, washing the cold away, but not the dread in the pit of your stomach. You can't stop thinking about whether you're doing the right thing.

What choice do I have?

Stepping out of the shower, eyes full of lather, groping for the towel, you placed it within easy reach. Wiping the soap away, Richard is in the doorway, the towel in his hand.

A cold spasm slithers down your back.

'Uh, could I have the towel, please?'

'I see your clothes are on the floor. There's a basket.' He prods the wet clothes with his foot, still holding onto the towel.

'Can I...?' He throws it towards you, turns and leaves without another word. Wrapping it around your waist, you fight back tears.

What have I done?

You hear him banging in the kitchen, then shouting, 'Dinner's nearly ready. How about helping?' Pulling on a dry T-shirt and a pair of shorts, you reluctantly go into the kitchen. Richard is all smiles, handing you knives and forks, his fingers brush your wrist. 'Hurry up, we don't want dinner going cold, do we, dear boy?' He's relaxed during dinner, talking about himself, the restaurant, and his life in Sydney. He mentions Oxford Street. 'Do you know where that is?' Shaking your head, no idea what he's talking about. He pauses, takes a deep breath and mumbles, 'You understand that I like men, don't you?' You eye your plate. 'Is that a problem?' You shake your head, eyes still on the plate. Richard continues, 'Tell me your story. How did you end up in my restaurant?'

Relieved that he's changed the subject, you break into a lengthy explanation of the trip and meeting Kevin. But avoid mentioning the police or the fact that Kevin has disappeared.

'Won't someone miss you?'

'I doubt it. No one cares.'

'I'm sure that's not true. You can stay for a few nights, until you sort something out.' He stands and walks around the table, his index finger trailing across the surface. Stopping behind you and picking up your plate, his breath warm against your cheek.

Pulling away, you blurt out, 'Let me do the dishes. I can do that.'

Richard titters. 'That's right. You're a dishwasher.'

Debating whether you can slink off to bed after you finish the washing up, deciding you can't, you join him in the lounge room.

After all, he is helping me.

He's seated on the lounge, the cat on his lap. 'Sorry about earlier. I find it stressful having a young man under my roof.' Fanning himself with his hand, 'I'd rather have him under me.' He pushes the cat off and slides towards you.

Your throat closes; it's hard to breathe.

No, not again.

You stutter, 'Should, should I... I go?'

Shaking his head, 'No. I like the company.' His leg presses against yours. 'I get lonely.' The pressure increases.

Moving away, you mumble, 'I can't. Sorry, I...'

'Very well. Time for bed. There's a spare front-door key on the table.'

Climbing into bed, you're glad he left you alone. The queasiness in your stomach begins to ease. *Maybe this will work out. But I can't, couldn't...* Sighing. *I've gotta find Kevin.*

The door opens, a sliver of light from the hallway spilling into the room. Richard stands in the doorway. You can see the tension in his body, taut like a violin string, his erection obvious. 'I like you,' he whispers, 'I think you owe me something, you know, for helping you out.'

'I never...' You stop, a lump in your throat.

'What if you let me suck you off?'

Should I? He's helping me.

Gritting your teeth. 'I... I can't.' His shoulders slump. He stares for a minute as if deciding what to do next. 'I'm away this weekend. Stay until then.' Then turns on his heel.

You want to explain, even say yes. Instead, stammering. 'I'm... I can't...' The door closes with a bang.

Refection: Guilt

> *"We must let go of the life we have planned, so as to accept the one that is waiting for us."* — Joseph Campbell

Guilt develops when we are blamed for actions as a child, even when we aren't at fault. As with all inner child wounds, guilt develops due to lack of love, care, and support. We put other people's needs first and feel guilty if we don't. Ordinary guilt is essential in modifying our behaviour and understanding when we do something wrong. However, when guilt is trauma-induced, it changes our behaviour. It's about how we see ourselves and how we think others see and value us. The guilt wound transforms us from thinking about what is best for us to what we can do for someone else. We no longer believe we deserve anything good and feel responsible for things that are not our responsibility. Once we believe that we are not loved, we become desperate for attention, approval, and praise. It's not a passing phase; we crave this as children and continue to do so as adults.

Caregivers will use guilt for control by what they say, not just what they do. For example, 'I've done everything for you, and you behave like that,' or 'If you were a good child, you'd listen.' My mother had a knack for making me feel responsible for her emotions. She'd say, 'Why don't you listen? You make everything difficult.' or 'Wait until your father gets home.'

An absence of love in childhood means we commence a lifelong search for the unattainable, perfect love. It then reinforces the belief that we're not loveable. Our guilt then grows and damages our decision-making as adults, as it did in childhood. The most common guilt wounds are:

- *Feeling inadequate.*

- *Frightened of getting into or being in trouble.*

- *Worried about being abandoned or rejected.*

- *Feeling bad even when we achieve success.*

- *Having a need to be liked or accepted by everyone we meet.*

- *Blaming ourselves for any inconvenience caused to others.*

Guilt continues to burden us as we grow into adults. We feel an overwhelming responsibility for other people's emotions and well-being. If not addressed, our guilt will shape our self-worth for the rest of our lives, leading to emotional exhaustion.

Adult Reaction: Needing Love

When I recall that moment with Richard, I remember how difficult it was to say no. My heart was in my mouth, and my whole body screamed, 'Say yes!' It's what I knew: submission. After he left, I lay awake for hours, feeling guilty for saying no.

Guilt is an insidious trauma. We feel responsible for everything, including our abuse. We become convinced we did something wrong. We may feel guilty about every pleasure we want or experience for the remainder of our lives. We've become so accustomed to the fact that we don't deserve anything.

I fell in love with a younger woman after my divorce. While we were together, my inner child was fulfilled, at peace and happy, as was I. Due to circumstances, we had to part. I was left hurt and feeling abandoned. My response was to curl up on the floor, physically sick with pain, feeling my heart tearing in two. I took a position in another town to escape the painful environment. However, my wounded inner child was in so much pain that the guilt of not being loved continued to haunt me. Ultimately, this guilt played out when I lost my job. As abused children in adult bodies, our needs and desire for love are as fundamental as breathing. Because of our guilt and underlying shame, many believe we deserve punishment even when something is not our fault. It can lead to seeking out situations that provide punishment, such as BDSM or fetishes. These give us the feeling of unworthiness that we developed as children.

Most of our lives have been spent believing danger is everywhere. We become hypersensitive to everyone's needs and feel guilty if we can't help. It will cause feelings of anxiety and low self-worth as we tell ourselves it's our fault. When guilt consumes us, we question whether we should be in this world.

Healing Exercise: Forgiving

Healing is about supporting and loving our inner child. In the following exercise, we'll write to our caregivers from our inner child. It's important to remember that what happened was not our fault. Begin by writing a letter to your father and then another to your mother. Tell them how you feel about what they did and didn't do for you and what you needed and never received. Be honest and open. No one will see these letters. Dispose of them as soon as you finish reading them.

Mine went like this: Dad, I needed your protection. I wanted you to love me and hold me when I was sad. I ached for you to tell me that you were proud of me. Instead, you beat me or, worse, ignored me. I only wanted to know that you cared and were happy I was in your life. But you never showed me that.

Mum, you stood by and watched the beatings. You fought with him for your voice but never for mine. Why not?

If any of these exercises trigger feelings of distress or reopen past traumas, seek professional help. It's not a sign of weakness but a worthwhile step on your healing journey.

There was relief in escaping Richard's clutches, but I felt guilty and a new emotion: fear of being alone in a strange city. Another twist brings welcome news until I realise I must do something I don't want to. Fear no longer drives me — it defines me. What does that mean as an adult? We'll find out in the next chapter.

Chapter Thirteen

Shadow of Fear

Was it a flash of red? Maybe you're seeing things. Rushing out of the station, stopping in Elizabeth Street.

Could it be Kevin?

There's nothing to suggest it was. For a fleeting moment, you believed your problems were over — no more Richard, no more being alone. How Kevin might help is unclear, but you believe he will.

It's gotta be him.

Bumping into an elderly man who gives you a withering look, you mumble an apology, and with a final glance along Elizabeth Street, prepare to go back to Richard.

Something strikes you on the back of the head as a familiar voice rings out. 'Where have you been?'

Turning around, mouth open, screaming, 'Kevin!' You wrap him in a bear hug.

'Easy, you'll crush me.'

Embarrassed, you step back, studying him at arm's length. His blonde hair in a familiar tangle, his top hat dangling from his left hand. 'I didn't think I'd ever see you again.' A weight lifts from your shoulders.

'I would've come sooner but...' A rueful smile crosses his face. 'I couldn't go near the Palace.'

'You're here now, that's all that matters. The bastards kicked me out.' Kevin, ashen-faced, 'What? Why?'

'They reckon I had something to do with... You know.' The police grabbed me and looked at my room.'

A pained expression crossed your face remembering being marched through the Palace foyer. 'They warned me to stay away from you. Then the prick in charge said I gotta go. Geez, I'm glad you're back.'

Shaking his head, 'I'm sorry. I went into the wrong room; this old bird began screaming at the top of her lungs...' He paused. 'I shit myself and ran. I went back after the hag in the booth left and got my stuff.' Kevin glanced around and leaned closer. 'But I've got good news.'

'What? What news?'

'I'm staying in a boarding house, and there's a bed for you if you want it.'

You grab him and shake his arm. 'What? How? Tell me?'

Kevin, finger to his lips. 'Shhh. Come over here.'

You huddle together in the shelter of a building, whispering like conspirators.

'Where is this place?'

'Jesus. Stop shaking my arm and I'll tell you.'

Sheepishly, you let go. 'Well?'

He grins. 'It's a boarding house for boys like us, with nowhere to go. It's in Lakemba. I told the lady who runs it about you and she said there's room for you. It's thirty-five dollars a week.'

His words tumble out too fast for you to follow. When he mentions the money, your shoulders sag. 'I ain't got that.'

'Can you get it?'

The television-room man's proposal flickers in the back of your mind. 'Who's gonna give me money?' Then you recall Reg's parting words.

Did he mean it? Smiling, you look at Kevin. 'I might be able to.'

'You're not thinking about that old prick from the Palace, are you?'

'Fuck off, I'm not stupid.'

'Yes, you are. What then?'

'We met this bloke on the way to Sydney. His name's Reg. He said I should go see him if I needed anything. He works at... umm, shit.'

Burying your head in your hands. *Shit where was it?* 'I can't remember.'

'Did he tell you a street, or anything about it, where he lived, worked?'

'Yes, where he worked. Said he had his dream job making beer, and I'd find him at a pub nearby, bell something.'

Kevin looks thoughtful. 'A brewery?'

'Maybe.'

'I've heard of Resch's brewery, in Redfern. Can't be that many pubs near it. Let's go see Betty. Don't tell her you ain't got the money. Tell her you're getting it from a friend.'

If only Reg can help. You don't want to ask Richard; that would mean payment of another kind.

***

Arriving at Lakemba Station, Kevin leads the way up Haldon Street. The houses here are all built from the same red brick. Toys, broken furniture and other rubbish lying in the dirt in their front yards. Kevin points out landmarks, assuming you'll be living here — you're not so sure. He points to a park, a rusting merry-go-round and broken metal slide in the yellowing grass. 'Kids hang out there at night, I'd avoid it.'

Everything's a blur, worried you'll get your hopes up and then won't get the money.

Kevin doesn't notice and continues in his newfound role as tour guide. 'There's a Chinese takeaway on Canterbury Road,' he says, adding, 'It's a cheap place to eat.' He hesitates outside a fruit and veg corner shop. Looking around, then moving closer to the boxes of fruit on the pavement, slipping an apple into his pocket, 'Watch out for the man inside. He'll come out yelling if he sees you.' He turns into a laneway alongside the shop. 'C'mon.' Taking a bite out of the apple, mouth full. 'It's down here.' At the end of the lane, throwing the apple core on the ground, he points across the street. 'That's it.'

It looks like all the others: red brick, low concrete front wall separating the yard from the street. The only feature, a veranda with blue and white timber railing surrounding it. An overstuffed fifties-style lounge with rolled arms takes up most of the veranda; you can't tell what colour, more dirt than anything else.

Kevin marches through the open front door. You follow, a shiver of delight running up your arms. Over his shoulder, Kevin mouths, *It'll be alright.*

The hallway is covered in a threadbare carpet, floral wallpaper peeling at the edges smothers the walls. Peeking into an open archway: three iron beds in the room, another room beyond holds more beds. One door is firmly secured by a solid brass padlock. Kevin mutters, 'That's Betty and Steve's room. No one goes in there.' At the end of the hallway, with a cheeky grin you're starting to recognise, he pushes open a glass-panelled door and strolls in.

The first thing you notice is the size of the rectangular table in the middle of the room, with mismatched timber chairs around it, one of them occupied by a boy.

A large bay window overlooks an unkempt rear garden. Two faded brown armchairs are pushed up against a wall, facing a television. Another boy lounges in one, legs splayed, his arms covered in blue-ink tattoos. He turns, looks, then turns away. The boy at the table shouts, 'Kevin's in trouble.'

'Hi, Alfie.' Out of the side of his mouth, Kevin whispers, 'Don't worry about Alfie, he always shouts.'

'Kevin's in trouble,' Alfie repeats in a loud voice.

The aroma of frying onions fills the air, reminding you that it's been a while since you've eaten. There's a clatter of dishes and cursing from what you assume is the kitchen. 'Hi Betty,' Kevin yells, pushing aside a set of multicoloured plastic strips to let you enter; they slither and hiss back into place.

A woman in a faded house coat, with a brightly coloured terry towelling cloth wrapped around her head, faces the stove, flour-covered hands on her hips. She turns around, sweat rolling down her face, grimacing. 'You're back then.'

'Yes, and I found Graham, the friend I told you about.'

She brushes away a wisp of hair, leaving a smudge of flour on her forehead. 'Nice to meet you, Graham.' She beckons for you to come closer. Her eyes soften, her mouth crinkling into a smile. 'So, you want to move in?'

Kevin grins. 'He does.'

Betty sniffs. 'Thank you, Kevin. Graham can answer for himself. Do your parents know where you are?'

Nodding, 'Yes, they, they're okay.' You recount the trip, leaving out a few things.

Her eyes remain focused on you, then, with a sigh, she turns back to the stove and lifts a frying pan off the heat. 'Let's try it for two weeks. Rent's thirty-five dollars a week... in advance. I provide breakfast and dinner on weekdays, and breakfast and lunch on weekends. No smoking, swearing or fighting in the house. You got the money?'

Hesitating, remembering Kevin's words, 'Uh, a friend has promised to give me the money. I'm gonna get it.'

'I'm going with him,' Kevin adds.

'That'll help,' she says, no hint of a smile on her face. 'I've got one bed available. It's yours if you come back with the rent money by tomorrow.'

'I will, I will.' But you're not sure.

Kevin practises more of his tour guide expertise on the way out of the house. 'That's your bed,' pointing to one near the entrance to the second room. 'Mine's at the foot of yours. George sleeps around the corner. You'll meet him and the others later.'

If I find Reg, and if he'll lend me the money. 'We'd better go and see Reg.' Kevin nods. 'Yeah. Okay.'

Back on a train, wanting to know more about the boy with the tattoos, you press Kevin. 'Who is he? He looked scary.'

'Neal? Nah. He's great. He's the only one with a single room, off the dining room. A friend of Betty's husband, Steve, both are from New Zealand.'

'Who else lives there?'

'You met Alfie. You can't talk to him; he only mutters or yells. Terry, he's the one who told me about the place.' He pauses as the train rattles and sways from side to side. 'Terry's family lives in Sydney, but they don't want to see him. Betty has a soft spot for him, though. Peter, he walks with a limp, doesn't say much, and Des, watch out for him, he can be a bastard. The other boy in our room is George. He's Greek, difficult to understand sometimes, but he's okay. Walks around without a shirt on, flexing his muscles.' He stops, looks out the window.

'Is something wrong?'

'See those chimneys? I think that's the brewery. C'mon, here's the station.'

Redfern is busy, people hurrying off the train and dashing through the turn-stiles, pushing past the man collecting tickets — he doesn't ask for a ticket, which is just as well because you don't have one.

There are more dilapidated terrace houses here, windows boarded up. You take hold of Kevin's elbow. 'Should we be here?' Shrugging you off, he keeps walking. Staying close to him, finding yourself too close as he comes to a sudden halt, and you walk smack-bang into his back. 'Ouch.' Rubbing your nose, 'How about telling me when you're gonna stop.'

'This is it.'

'You sure?' Kevin nods.

The hotel sits on the corner of Redfern and Regent streets, and it's huge. It may have been beautiful once, but now the green and white tiles on the walls are cracked and covered in dust and dirt. 'Bellevue Hotel' on a sign above them.

'Where do we go? It's so big.'

Kevin points to a glass door with 'Public Bar' etched into it.

Hesitating, 'Can we go in?'

Lifting his shoulders, a brief look of annoyance on his face, 'If you wanna find this Reg, you have to. Anyway, we're here now.'

Shaking your head, 'I don't know if I can ask him for money.'

'Shit. He said he'd help, didn't he?'

'People say lots of stuff.' You wipe your palms down the front of your jeans. Then, summoning your courage, you enter.

Two men occupy one table, they glance in your direction and then return to their beers. Each takes a mouthful. The floor is sticky underfoot, like walking on flypaper, and there's an acrid smell of stale beer, making your nose twitch. The barman, a glass in one enormous paw, looks at you.

Kevin whispers, 'Do you see him?' A shake of your head. 'Ask the barman. If he's a regular, he'll know him.'

The idea of approaching the stout-looking barman, displeasure all over his face, doesn't fill you with joy.

Conscious of how you must look, long hair, torn jeans, you shuffle to the bar. Before you can open your mouth, he snaps, 'You kids shouldn't be in here. What do you want? C'mon, quick. I'll get in trouble if the boss sees you.'

'We're looking for someone. He drinks here. His name's Reg.'

The barman puts the glass down on the bar with a thump. 'Yeah, there's a Reg that drinks here. Wadda you want with him?'

Your spirits lift. 'Has he been in today?' The barman remains silent, still eyeing you, waiting for more. 'I met him after he'd been to a rodeo.'

He relaxes. 'Reg does love his rodeos.' Looking up at the clock, 'It's only two, and the brewery fellas knock off at four.' Grinning, 'He'll arrive five minutes later.'

A man seated on a stool in the corner swivels to face you. 'Reg tole me last night he'd got sum overtime. He'll be late.'

'Can I leave a message?'

'Ey what?' the barman says.

'A message, can I leave one?'

He nods, handing over a crumpled, beer-stained docket and a pencil, its end chewed to bare lead. Scribbling the message, you hand it back, folding it, he puts it in the till.

'You'll give it to him?'

'Yep. Now get out of here.'

Back on the street, turning to Kevin, 'What now?'

He has the impish grin again. 'I know a place where you can make money, if you're not too worried about what you do.'

Not knowing what he means, but a cold sensation settles in your stomach, suggesting you might not like what he's got in mind. 'What do you mean? Where is it?'

'It's easy if you...'

Annoyed, 'If you, what?'

Sniggering, 'C'mon. I'll show you.' Playfully pinching your arm, amusement sparkles in his eyes. 'It's called the Wall.' As you walk, he tells you about the Wall. The more you hear, the less you want to go. Kevin stops and looks around.

'Is this it, the Wall? Doesn't look like what you said.'

Shaking his head, Kevin points across the road. 'It's over there.' His breath rasps in his chest.

'You okay?'

'I...' He gasps, takes a deep breath. 'I'm okay.' He gives you a weak smile. 'It comes and goes.'

'Why are we here?'

'Money.'

You're expecting to come across a line of men, hands full of dollar notes. Instead, you see a Wall covered in drawings of impressive-sized cocks, phone numbers and meeting places. A young boy leans against the far end, tensing as he spies you. Lank, straw-coloured hair hangs down over his face, his wafer-thin legs sticking out of baggy shorts secured around his waist by a piece of rope. He glances at you once more and then hurries away.

Shaken, you turn to Kevin. 'We should leave.'

'Why? Don't you want to make some money?'

Letting out a long sigh, closing your eyes, unable to answer. You want money, but at what cost? You're not sure.

Hands shaking, you pull out the packet of Champion from your pocket. You'd snagged it from a man in the toilets at the railway station. Trembling, your fingers unable to roll a smoke. The Wall brought back memories of a man in Africa.

***

He lived in the flat one door down from my family. Whenever you went outside to play, he appeared, dressed in a faded red terry-towelling dressing gown. He never said a word, but after a few minutes, his dressing gown would fall open and flap around his white stubby legs. Without shifting his gaze, his hand, covered in a mass of black, curly hair, groped for his cock. His hand slid up and down the shaft until he had an erection. His breath ragged, as he stroked. Then he'd rush back inside his flat, slamming the door behind him. It was always the same.

***

Kevin's snort brought you back to the Wall. He scoffed. 'You're making a mess of that. It's all over the pavement.'

'Give me a break.'

'Pass it here. My dad smoked rollies, loved his Drum, and he showed me how to roll, when Mum wasn't looking.' A wistful look crosses his face, quickly disappearing. 'Here.'

Lighting up and inhaling, calming yourself.

Can I do this? If Reg doesn't give me the money, what else is there?

As if on cue, a car pulls up at the curb, the driver sits motionless, staring straight ahead. Whispering to Kevin, 'What's he doing?'

Kevin grins. 'Wait.'

'For what?'

'Shhh.'

'Have you...?'

Kevin hesitates, watching the car. 'Yeah, I let an old fart suck me off. He gave me ten bucks. Cheap bastard.'

The driver crooks a finger in your direction. Kevin elbows you in the ribs. 'Go and see what he wants.'

Shaking your head, 'This is stupid.'

Another strike to your ribs. 'Go on.'

'Stop that.'

'Do you wanna move in or not?'

Grinding what's left of the soggy rollie into the pavement, blanching, you walk towards the car, a sour taste filling your mouth. Nearing the open window, your nostrils fill with the odour of Brut covering a rancid smell of sweat. The man leans across, his fingers covered in coarse black hair. 'How, how much?' he croaks, his pants unzipped, a flaccid white cock pokes out.

Unable to control the trembling, stuttering, 'F-f-for what?'

He takes it in his hand. 'To suck this.'

Shaking your head, 'I don't. I can't.'

Baring his teeth, 'How much to suck you? Get in. I'll make it worth your while.'

'No... I don't,' recoiling, tripping over your own feet, nearly landing flat on your back.

'You prick teaser. Fuck you,' he screamed. The car roared away, tyres squealing, smoke belching from its exhaust as it veered into traffic.

There's a cackle and snort behind you. Over your shoulder, you see Kevin clutching his belly, face contorted in glee.

'What's so funny?'

'You,' he gurgles. 'I've never seen anyone move backwards that fast.' He performs an impression of you tripping over your own feet.

'Fuck off. I'm never coming back here.'

Breaking into another fit of giggles, dropping to his knees, Kevin pleads for you to stop. Clenching your hands, you step towards him. Taking a deep breath, he gets himself under control and glances at your hands, raising his palms. 'Okay, okay.'

Chest heaving. 'What now?'

Kevin wipes the tears from his eyes. 'Let's go to the Cross, it isn't far. Unless you wanna try again?'

Furious, you walk away. The smile is gone as he joins you. 'C'mon, I'm only kidding. Also, you're going the wrong way.'

Your anger isn't directed at him but at yourself, ashamed at what you might have to do. You don't want to return to Darwin.

But does it mean I have to do that?

You're excited about King's Cross. You've heard of the gangsters who frequent the place and prostitutes who offer their bodies to those who want them. Pictures of seedy characters lurking in dark alleyways fill your head.

It's nothing like it. The people strolling the streets resemble office workers, not underworld figures. They carry briefcases, not guns or drugs. Others, dress like your dad in safari suits. Girls mince past in miniskirts and midriff tops, mixing with middle-aged ladies in their finest clothing, weighed down by designer bags. The only seediness you can see are strip clubs squeezed between banks and butchers, but no one cares as they go about their business.

A boy thrusts a copy of the *Daily Mirror* into your hands. 'It's yours,' he yells. Waving him away, laughing that he thinks you have money for a newspaper. You're envious of a man passing by in brown velvet bell-bottoms and matching vest over a white T-shirt. He sports a wide-brimmed hat, worn at an angle on his head, giving him a refined air.

Kevin gawks at pictures of girls at the entrance to a place called 'Pink Panther'. He squints, shading his eyes from the sun, whispering, 'Think we can get in?'

The bouncer, on the front step, calls out to passers-by: 'Come in. Come in. Best girls in Sydney. The show's about to begin.' Most avert their gaze and hurry past.

He glances at Kevin, who's still gawping at the pictures. 'Move along, kid. Come back when you've got hair around your balls.' His stomach strains against a black frilled shirt, two buttons have popped open. Rolls of neck fat spill over his collar. 'Go on, piss off,' he mutters under his breath.

With a firm grip on Kevin's arm, you drag him away — you've had enough of angry men.

A girl with thick black eyeshadow and glossy pink lips smiles as you pass. 'Don't worry about him boys, he's a shithead.' She wipes her hands down her arms, brushing away some imagined problem. With a cackle, 'If you boys want fun, come back and see me?' We rush past as she screeches at our retreating backs, 'I'll do both of you.' You've found the King's Cross you've heard of.

Kevin's breathing is ragged. You help him to a bench, worried he might collapse as a cough racks his chest. 'Will you be okay?' He nods. Moving away, keeping one eye on him, you roll a cigarette. The smoke catches in your throat and you start coughing. You hear Kevin muttering that you sound like him. Throwing the smoke away. You help him up. 'We can't be too long. I don't wanna miss Reg.'

Kevin looks better as you cross the road, arm in arm.

The Cross is different here. Out of sight of the public, the buildings are dirtier; rubbish piled up on the pavement. Two girls in a doorway look in your direction. They exchange nods, and one takes a step towards you. 'Got a light, luv?' A gold skirt highlights her pale legs, red blotches on her knees. Thick makeup can't cover a damaged face. With a whine, 'Well, got a light for a girl or not?'

You fumble for your matches; a cloying, sweet perfume engulfs you. She takes them and strikes one, lighting her cigarette, sucking in a lungful of smoke, tucking the matchbox between her breasts. 'Thanks, luv. Would you like something special?' She winks and looks over her shoulder at her friend. Bending forward, her breasts try to free themselves from her top. 'We'll give you a good time, both of you,' she hoots.

When you don't accept, she glances at Kevin, and then, with a sniff, turns and walks back to her friend, hips swaying from side to side.

Heading back to Bellevue, praying Reg will lend you the money, your fingernails chewed to the wick by the time you arrive. It's the moment of truth, and you're not sure you want to find out. Your confidence ebbs away as your mind fills with doubt.

What if he's not here, or worse, won't lend me the money?

Kevin groans. 'What's wrong now?'

'I don't… What if he can't? If he doesn't lend me the money?'

Kevin puts an arm around your shoulder. 'If he's not here, then we'll go back to the Wall together and make the money.'

'You'd… you'd really do that… for me?'

'Shit yeah.'

Taking a deep breath, you know you have to find out, and buoyed by Kevin's words, you enter the pub. The same two men are at their table, nursing beers. The only other occupants are a man and a woman, deep in conversation. But no Reg. A different barman is wiping the top of the bar. Looking up, he scowls. 'Kids aren't allowed in here.'

You open your mouth to ask about Reg, snapping it shut as he strolls into the bar, his face breaking into a smile. 'Graham, good to see you again,' wrapping his brawny arms around you. He hasn't changed a bit, the sweat-stained Akubra still jammed on his head. 'I got your note. Plenty of beer here, so I didn't mind waiting. Who's your friend?' You introduce Kevin. 'Would you like a drink? Lemon squashes?' We sit at a corner table as Reg heads to the bar.

Kevin leans across. 'We have to be quick or we won't get back in time for dinner.'

'Now we have to be quick? Geez, he's lending me money. Wait.'

Reg returns with four drinks on a tray, two beers for him. 'Cheers,' he says, taking a gulp. 'Ah, that's good.' Reaching into his pocket, he pulls out an envelope and slides it across the table. 'Here you go.'

'I... don't. How? Thank you. I'll pay it back. I promise.'

He nods. 'I know you will, or I wouldn't lend it to you. There's a bit extra to tide you over.'

Kevin puts down his empty glass and begins fidgeting in his seat, his breathing shallow. He quickly huffs, 'We better go.'

Reg chuckles. 'Where's this place?'

'It's in Lakemba. I guess we'd better.' There's a tear in the corner of your eye as you stand and say goodbye. With a sniff, 'I...', struggling to find the words.

Reg waves you to silence. 'You helped me out. I'm glad I can return the favour. Funny how these things work out.'

Shaking hands, promising again that you'll pay him back as soon as you can.

Reflection: Fear

"Courage starts with showing up and letting ourselves be seen. Because true belonging only happens when we present our authentic, imperfect selves to the world, our sense of belonging can never be greater than our level of self-acceptance. Vulnerability sounds like truth and feels like courage." — Brené Brown

Our fears stem from the original shaming, not as a passing worry but as a sense of dread — even when there is no immediate danger. It's fear of abandonment, rejection, or not being good enough. We spend our childhood tiptoeing around our caregiver's behaviour and poor emotional responses. These fears can also manifest physically: clenched stomach, tight chest, flinching at sudden noises or conflict. It drives negative emotions like people-pleasing, avoidance, over-explaining, and feeling alone, no matter how many people surround us. These seem irrational to an adult but not to the inner child. It can't distinguish between what is real and what is not, so everything is dangerous. When challenged, it reacts like a wild animal roaring to frighten off a rival. It's the only way it can feel safe and take back control. Seemingly minor events can trigger our fear. It's about what was missing in our childhood: love, security, and reassurance.

As children, we learn from our caregivers; if they are poor role models, we grow up with no idea how to set personal boundaries. Not being taught them means we can't negotiate or discuss calmly and rationally, particularly when responding out of fear. However, not all of our responses are angry or violent. The other ways in which it impacts our lives including:

- *Keeping our distance to stay safe.*

- *Pushing people away to prevent being disappointed.*

- *Needing to achieve perfection to avoid criticism.*

- *Prioritising the needs of others over ourselves to avoid conflict.*

- *Wanting to control our relationships to avoid rejection.*

Recognising and understanding these fears can be a decisive step toward healing and growth.

Adult Reflection: Repressed Trauma

Would I have returned to the Wall if Reg had said no to giving me the money? The answer is yes. My fear of not being safe and having a home overrode all other concerns. Even if that meant doing something, I didn't want to. My time in Sydney was always a choice between the lesser of two evils.

As adults, we cope with our inner child's fear by keeping it separate from our reality, developing an impenetrable shell-like exterior. For most of my life, I've used humour, sarcasm and self-deprecating remarks to deflect any pain or hurt I might feel. Allowing my true feelings to surface when I'm alone. I missed out on many genuine friendships because of this. It wasn't a conscious decision to deny my feelings and pretend. It was a survival response. When all is well, we don't hear from our inner child. When threatened, its fear overwhelms us.

I think of our repressed trauma as removed from our adult emotions so we can have everyday interactions without issue. I imagine them as captured in a balloon. They may have been building towards eruption for years, particularly if we face an ongoing trigger within the home or workplace. Ultimately, it takes time for the emotion to erupt. For example, a partner constantly criticises us over a minor issue that brings back memory fragments of our abuse in childhood. One day, the trauma erupts in a violent and unrecognisable rage.

The following might explain. It is an extreme example and not necessarily the reaction of an angry, wounded inner child. It happened in a small rural town. A quiet and well-respected sixty-nine-year-old man took an axe and killed his wife and two grandchildren while babysitting them. His daughter arrived to collect the children and was also attacked but survived. The man then calmly left his home, went to a nearby town, went into a pub, sat down and ordered a beer.

I don't know what triggered such a violent reaction. Why did the reality of his actions not appear to affect him? Was he disconnected from that rage? There is no answer to these questions because when asked why he did it? He said, 'I don't know why myself.'

I cannot say that a raging, wounded inner child is the reason for this horrifying act. There are many reasons for people to act violently. However, whenever I hear a story like this, I always think about the possibility that early childhood trauma has unleashed its anger once more. Due to our childhood abuse, we all have the capacity for extreme rage if we don't take steps to heal.

Healing Exercise: Breathwork

By acknowledging our fear, we heal, grow, and bring a new sense of optimism to ourselves. It's our responsibility to address our inner child's fear and need for safety. One of the best ways we can achieve this is by paying close attention to it and providing love to ease its fear. Healing takes time, commitment, and, in most cases, professional therapy. We mustn't forget that our pain and hurt have been with us for many years, so proceed gently.

This exercise will bring a sense of calm and peace to your nervous energies and help you navigate problems without overreaction. I recommend undertaking it whenever you experience fear or anxiety. To start, find somewhere quiet and sit comfortably or lie down, whichever you prefer.

1. *Begin by breathing in and know you are breathing in — breathe out and know you are breathing out.*

2. *Bring your attention to the in-breath and then to the out-breath.*

3. *Breathe in, and be aware of your body — breathe out, and be aware of your body.*

4. *Now, as you breathe in, see yourself as a five-year-old child, fragile and vulnerable.*

5. *As you breathe out, imagine the five-year-old child smiling.*

6. *Now breathe in and be aware that this five-year-old child is you.*

7. *As you breathe out, imagine cuddling the five-year-old against your chest.*

We reclaim power over ourselves by recognising our inner child's fears and offering it the safety it craves.

Fresh from considering one lousy choice, another trauma is exposed: my need for constant reassurance. How is this going to affect me? Next, we explore insecure attachments, their meaning, and their impact on our relationships.

CHAPTER FOURTEEN

Dance of Doubt

Kevin hurried out of Lakemba Station. 'Betty's strict about meal times. She shuts the kitchen if you're late.'

You arrive to find Betty hovering over the stove. Wiping her brow, she beams at Kevin.

'I didn't think you'd miss dinner.' Glancing at you, 'Does this mean you're moving in, Graham?'

Nodding like an excited puppy, 'Yes, yes, I am,' handing over the money. She stuffs it down the front of her housecoat.

'Kevin, show Graham where he'll be sleeping. Dinner will be ready soon. Alfie, come and help set the table.'

Kevin takes the bag off your shoulder, and with a grin that's a mile wide, escorts you to the bed he showed you a few hours ago. 'George, we've got a new roommate.'

A bare-chested boy, blue singlet over his shoulder, stomps around the corner. 'This your friend?' His curly brown hair hangs to the middle of his back, he sweeps it away from his face and grins, 'Hope you don't mind noise. Kevin snores all night long.'

Kevin's smile fades. 'Shut up. I don't.'

'If it's not snoring, then it must be farting,' George says, smirking. His words roll together, making him difficult to understand.

You enjoy the joking between them, but the reality is you don't know how long you are staying. With a sigh, you mutter, 'I gotta find a job.'

'Betty said something about a job. Ask her. She'll take care of you,' George says, walking back around the corner.

Kevin introduces the others at dinner, they nod, then focus back on their food.

Except Des, his eyes hooded as he studies you, impossible to tell what he's thinking.

Betty, a bowl of steaming mashed potatoes in one hand, leans over your shoulder. 'The boys are going to a dance tonight. Why don't you go with them?'

Terry, putting his knife and fork down, 'Yeah, you should. There'll be lots of girls.'

'Girls, girls,' Alfie chants.

'Alfie, be quiet,' George snaps, ladling mash onto his plate.

Terry grins. 'You wanna come?'

Neal's eyes narrow. 'Be careful. There are Sharpies at those dances and they don't like long hairs.' Terry, George and Kevin all solemnly nod.

***

On the train, heading to the dance, you ask what Neal meant about the Sharpies. 'Kevin, are they the same as at the snooker place?'

He laughs and looks at Terry. 'You know more about Sharpies than me. Tell Graham about 'em.' Terry ignores him, which only makes him more insistent. 'C'mon, tell him.'

Terry, frowning, stares at you. 'You wanna know?' You nod. Sighing, he glances out the window. 'Stay away from them, is all you need to know.'

'Why don't they like long hair?'

Terry looks daggers at you. 'They don't need a reason. They hate blond-haired surfies as well, like you, Kevin.' He sniffs. 'But everyone is fair game.' Then, with a shake of his head, he mutters, 'Make sure you don't go near their brushs.'

'They carry brushes?'

Terry studies you as if you're making fun of him. 'Brushs are their chicks. They belong to 'em. Now shut up, we're nearly there.'

Terry leads the way out of Campsie Station. Kevin wants to take a shortcut through the park, but Terry shakes his head. 'It's not a good idea.'

Kevin is about to argue, until a look from George makes him decide otherwise. Instead, grasping Terry by the arm, dragging him along to hurry him up. Terry, grumbling, shoves him away. 'What's your hurry?'

'I don't wanna miss any of the fun.' Seeing the long line to get into the hall, Kevin moans, 'I told you.'

Inside, you force your way through the packed bodies, finding an unoccupied piece of wall from which to watch the rolling wave of bodies all moving as one to the beat. Coloured lights pulsate from big black boxes on the stage, casting a spooky glow. Kevin shouts that he's going to look around and disappears into the crowd.

Terry elbows you. Wincing, you turn to him; he motions toward a corner where four boys are dancing, their arms and legs flailing in wild gyrations. It gives you the impression of a fight more than a dance. One of them, who appears to be their leader, is wearing sailor pants with braces over a polo shirt buttoned up to his neck.

Terry whispers, 'See 'em?' You nod. 'I know one. Stay well clear.'

Why would I go near them?

Looking away, concentrating on the girls spinning on the dance floor, worried that you haven't seen Kevin for a while. Then he appears, startling you.

This dance is stupid. Do you wanna leave?' He tugs on Terry's shirtsleeve, 'You coming?' Terry shakes his head. George is nowhere to be seen, but he can look after himself.

You fail to notice that the Sharpies are no longer in the corner.

Outside, punching Kevin on the shoulder, you laugh. 'I didn't meet any girls. What about you?'

Kevin mutters, 'I didn't like any of them.'

'Bullshit, you like 'em all. They don't like you.'

With his arm around your neck, he shouts, 'Fuck off.'

You wrestle each other like two drunks, yelling and laughing at the top of your voices, staggering from side to side across the road. Panting, Kevin stops. 'C'mon, we can cut through the park. It'll save time.'

Getting your breath back, shaking your head, 'Terry didn't think it was a good idea.'

'He's not here.'

At the paved entrance to the park, staring into the inky blackness. 'Kevin, are you sure about this?'

'Don't be chicken. It's okay.'

With a determined air, he starts along the path, and, as is becoming your habit, you follow.

The glow from the streetlights fades, a noise in the bushes raises the hairs on the back of your neck.

Grasping Kevin's shoulder, 'I think we should go back.'

A *crunch* behind, faint. Swivelling around, nothing. Moving alongside Kevin, 'Did you hear that?'

You can't see his face but there's scorn in his voice. 'Get a grip. C'mon, it's not far.'

A piercing whistle rips through the night. Stopping, unsure of what's happening. 'Kevin, Kevin, what… what was that?'

He looks left and right, voice wavering. 'I, I don't, I can't…'

Peering into the dark, you can't see anything. Gripping his forearm, 'Should, should we keep going?' Another whistle, this time closer.

'Shit!' Kevin exclaims.

Glancing in the direction he's looking, your heart skips a beat, the sharpie in sailor pants is standing in the centre of the path. Raising a hand to his lips, he emits a short, sharp whistle, a signal. There's rustling in the trees, branches crack. Eyes wide, you watch Sharpies drop one after another to the ground.

Kevin screams, 'Run, run, for fuck's sake run!'

Racing through the bushes, ignoring the whipping stems, trying to get away from the Sharpie in sailor pants as he attempts to cut you off, his pants slow him down. In frustration, he yells, 'Get the cunts. Get 'em!' There's a thud and a moan behind you, but you're not turning around to look.

Kevin is ahead, shouting.

You can't make out what he's saying.

Struggling to breathe, your body is cold as you burst out of the park onto the street, lit from the pale-yellow glow of a single streetlight. With relief, you spot the railway station.

A panicked scream from Kevin. 'The train's arriving. Shit, shit, we're gonna miss it.'

Mustering what strength you have left, legs pumping like pistons, you run. The Sharpies are nowhere to be seen.

Where are they?

You hurdle the turnstile, stumbling, falling to one knee.

'Get up, get up. They're coming,' Kevin screams from an open carriage. 'Hurry.'

You glance back to see sailor pants climbing over the turnstile. The bottom of his trouser leg catches on a turnstile arm, and he tumbles to the ground.

Kevin screams, 'Jump.' Launching yourself across the platform, you dive headfirst into the carriage as the train begins to move out of the station.

The Sharpies gather around the boy on the ground, one stares after you, dragging a finger across his throat.

Full of bravado, now you're on a moving train, you and Kevin gesture with raised fingers.

Kevin, gasping, sits and wipes his face, but he's smiling, as if it's all a game. Shivering, you think about the mayhem if they'd made it onto the train.

Not gonna tell Kevin how scared I am.

Pulling your knees up to your chest, hoping this is your last encounter with Sharpies. Little do you know.

***

You wake with a start. Sharpies drag you off a train, kicking and stomping. Sitting up, glancing around your room, you relax, breathing easier, waiting for the trembling to ease. You think about the job Betty has arranged.

What if I stuff it up?

Slipping out of bed, tiptoeing to the dining room, shivering even though it's a warm evening. A round moon casts shadows across the room. Turning to go back to bed, Neal is standing in front of his bedroom door, arms folded across his chest. A scraping comes from inside his room, a fleeting shadow under the door.

Did I imagine that? Must have. We're not allowed.

Flexing his fingers, stepping towards you, hissing, 'Why are you creeping around the house at night?'

'I'm, I'm not. I couldn't sleep.'

'You up to summit?'

'No. The job, I…'

With a slow smile, he relaxes. 'Betty doesn't like anyone wandering around the house at night. Betta get to bed.'

'Sure, sure.' You glance again at his door, the light underneath, now a solid beam.

I must have imagined it.

His eyes bore into you as you leave.

***

The morning after the dance, Betty taps you on the shoulder. 'I've got good news. A friend of mine needs an extra pair of hands in his factory, starting Monday. It's near Punchbowl Road, so you'll have to catch a bus. Steve can show you. He goes that way.'

'I… I… uh… don't know what to say. Thanks.' She smiles as she fiddles with the scarf around her head. Kevin winks.

The bus pulls away, leaving you in an industrial area, padlocked doors and barred windows on every building. There's a downtrodden, grittiness about the area, reminding you of Pitt Street. Wilson's Joinery is set back from the road, sandwiched between Johnson's Panel Beaters and an electronics shop offering free installation for every Rank Arena television purchased.

Sliding a glass door open, stepping into a cubicle, a girl behind a desk doesn't bother looking up, instead continues to admire her fingernails under the light of a desk lamp.

'Hi. I'm, uh, I'm Graham. Here for, uh, Betty said...'

Startled, quickly hiding her hand, the girl glares. An irritated expression crosses her face. 'What? Betty? Betty who?'

'She said she'd, uh, she'd arranged work for...'

'Oh. You're the kid Dad mentioned this morning. He's not here. Eric's the supervisor. He'll get you started.'

She stands, her chair smacking against the wall, and stalks towards a door marked 'Staff Only'. It opens to a thundering noise of hammering, drilling and sawing, a physical punch to your chest, but it doesn't bother her. She motions to a man gesturing at two others.

Hurling the paper that he's waving under their noses onto a bench, he stomps over, hands thrust deep in his blue overalls.

'What you want?'

The girl, visibly shaken by his manner, 'He's, Dad said, he...' She nods at you. 'He's starting today.'

He looks at you, then back at her. 'He didn't say nuthin to me.'

'Well, he's here.'

Fixing his eyes on you again, 'You can work this?' He waves a hand at the workshop.

Shaking your head, he mutters under his breath, throws his hands in the air and storms off.

One of the men who'd been in discussion with him wanders over with a friendly smile. Black spots cover his cheeks.

'Sharon, everything okay?' Sighing, she repeats what she told the other man. He laughs. 'I'll take care of it.' Sticking out his hand, 'I'm Gary. What's your name?'

'Uh, Graham.'

'Don't worry about Eric. He gets cranky, but he's okay most of the time. Let's kit you out and then get you started. There'll be overalls in the storeroom.' He looks you up and down, sizing you up. 'I reckon we'll have something that'll fit you. You'll need boots too.'

You glance down — there's a hole in one of your shoes.

Sharon walks away without a word, slamming the door behind her.

Gary grins and leads you across the workshop, past benches stacked with furniture in various stages of assembly. Taking a deep breath, hesitating, as Gary enters a storeroom. He looks over his shoulder and says, 'C'mon.' Palms sweating, you step inside. Gary pulls a box off a shelf and digs through it, letting out a loud snort, he holds up a pair of overalls. 'Told ya. These'll work a charm. Get changed in the loo.' The overalls smell of sweat and sawdust, but they fit, as does the pair of old boots he gives you. 'Alright. Now, what can you do?'

'Um. I've worked in a laundry.'

'Not much call for that here. Let's start you on something easy.' He takes you over to the buzz-saw. The man operating it sees you approaching and switches off the machine; then places his hands in the crook of his back and stretches, a frown on his face. 'Brett, meet Graham, he's starting today. I'm gonna get him to carry the sawn timber to the benches, okay?' Brett grunts, turns away and starts up the saw again. Hands over his ears, Gary yells, 'You'll get used to it.'

An hour later, arms numb, nose and throat filled with sawdust, you're jolted by a loud whistle reverberating through the workshop.

Alarmed, dropping the timber, it bangs against your shins before crashing to the floor. Everyone heads to a door at the rear of the workshop. Gary, laughing, helps you pick up the timber. 'Put it over here,' he says, holding the last piece. 'That old prick Eric should be happier. You've helped speed up the work. C'mon, smoko time.'

A blue haze fills the room, everyone is seated around the one table, cigarettes in hand, sipping from steaming cups.

Gary points to a kitchenette. 'Help yourself. There's coffee and tea.' A tin of instant coffee sits alongside a bubbling urn. A timber shelf holds assorted chipped cups and a plastic container marked 'Sugar' in black biro. The whistle blows again. 'Finish your coffee, Graham, then wash up,' Gary yells as he departs.

Within a few days, you begin to feel comfortable around the men. They laugh and tease you good-naturedly, and in a strange twist, you've become the dishwasher after each smoko.

Gary moves you to fixing cloth to the bases of lounge frames with a stapling gun. He changes his mind after you staple your fingers to a timber frame, suggesting glue instead — much safer.

Friday morning, as you leave for work, Betty shouts, 'Graham, don't forget your rent's due tonight.'

That afternoon, Gary yells, 'Pay time.' He slaps you on the back, propelling you towards the queue outside the door to the front office.

Sharon is there — it's the first time you've seen her since you began. In her hands is a box of yellow envelopes and a sheet of paper. When each man's name is called, they go up, take their envelope, then sign the sheet of paper. When Sharon calls your name, you take the envelope, your fingers brush against hers, but she doesn't notice, instead mutters, 'Sign here,' tapping the sheet with a red fingernail.

Gary puts an arm around your shoulders. 'Hey, we're heading to the pub. Are you coming?' Undecided, knowing you must get back and pay the rent, until he turns to Sharon. 'How about you Shaz?'

She nods. 'Yep.'

Rent forgotten, 'I'll come.'

Gavin is closest in age to you; he and Sharon spend the night whispering to each other; she doesn't look in your direction. Gavin invites everyone back to his flat to play cards, but you think there's another reason. At Gavin's, you lie on the lounge, sneaking occasional glances at Sharon. Your eyelids close. Sitting up, wide-eyed.

Where am I?

Oh, that's right, Sharon. But everything is quiet. There's no one else in the room. Panicked, you see the clock shows seven, and you know it means seven in the morning.

Fuck. Rent. What will she do?

Racing to catch the bus, stomach churning. You need Betty to trust you, and this wasn't going to help. You pray.

Please don't kick me out. Please.

Sprinting down the hallway into the dining room, coming to a shuddering halt. Kevin and Terry are at the table finishing breakfast. Both grin at the worried look on your face. Kevin, with a snigger, 'You're in trouble.'

'What, what did...?'

'Betty took your stuff and locked it in her room.'

'Shit. What...?'

Kevin suggests, 'Hide in the kitchen and then jump out and surprise her.'

In a low voice, Terry says, 'She's coming.'

You can't think of anything else to do, so you duck into the kitchen. Kevin, always ready to do something silly, joins you.

'You finished?' Betty says to Terry, marching into the lounge room.

Terry, with a mouthful of cornflakes, mumbles, 'Nearly.'

'Good.' She strides into the kitchen without glancing left or right.

'Hey Betty!' Kevin shouts, 'Look who I found!'

Betty jumps, pressing her hands against her chest. 'Kevin, don't, you'll give...' She stops, her lips forming a thin line. 'Graham. What did I say about rent being due on Fridays?'

Your heart sinks as you fight back tears. 'Sorry. They all went for a drink, and I lost track of time. I, I'm...'

A smile at the corner of her mouth, eyes twinkling, 'I'm gonna have a word with that boss of yours, taking a young 'un to the pub. I put your stuff in my room for safekeeping.'

'It won't happen again, I promise.'

Pulling the rent money out of your pocket.

She stuffs it down the front of her top. 'Everyone can make a mistake. Want some breakfast?'

'Yes, please.'

Kevin and Terry smile as Betty places an empty bowl on the table, squeezing your shoulder. Your heart swells at the touch. *I'm home.*

Reflection: Insecure Attachments

> *"Trauma is not what happens to you but what happens inside you."*
> — Gabor Maté

Insecure attachment is the feeling of being helpless and fearful in relationships, and an inability to have a healthy relationship. These feelings may go unrecognised until we stop to examine why our poor relationship behaviours keep recurring. As children from homes that lacked love, we develop a fear of rejection and abandonment, leading to insecure attachments. The most common of these are anxious-preoccupied, avoidant-dismissive and disorganised attachment. Of course, we can't heal what we don't understand. We can have good relationships. However, over time, we start to see patterns within our relationships and in the people we are attracted to. These tend to be negative. Let's look at the individual insecure attachments and how they affect us.

- ***Anxious attachment:*** *With this attachment, we want closeness and approval. We fear rejection or abandonment. This stops us from getting close to someone. With an anxious attachment, we need to be constantly reassured that our partner loves us.*

- ***Avoidant attachment:*** *With this attachment, we want independence in relationships. It leads to downplaying the need for emotional connection. We suppress emotions and struggle with intimacy and become emotionally distant or disconnected from our partners, and we're unable to explain why.*

- ***Disorganised attachment:*** Here, we combine anxious and avoidant attachments. We are unpredictable and struggle with intimacy and in maintaining long-term relationships. We desire to be close to someone, but because we fear that connection, we become emotionally distant from them.

Insecure attachments do not make for healthy and stable relationships. However, we can heal by acknowledging our behaviour and understanding that we must change. As I've said, we can't change what we don't know. Once we do know, we must change. Once we do, we can build secure attachments with higher self-esteem and better self-reliance, leading to a healthy relationship.

Adult Reaction: Loneliness

As adults, we continue to struggle with intimacy and genuine affection due to our insecure attachments. Attachment styles can impact us at different times. For example, disorganised attachment pulls us in two different directions at the same time. It leads to volatile relationships. One day, we are loving; the next, we are distant and appear aloof. I can attest to how frustrating this is for a partner because I've acted like this in past romantic relationships. I would be dependent and need constant reassurance that my partner wanted me. My need to be reassured was so great that it would lead to jealousy and controlling behaviour by me. Paradoxically, this pushes them away, leading to abandonment. I would rationalise my behaviour by blaming my partner and convincing myself it's their fault, not mine.

Insecure attachments don't stop at romantic relationships. They strain friendships as well. When I celebrated my twenty-first, I met some friends at a cocktail bar. I didn't tell them it was my twenty-first as I was embarrassed that I had few people to celebrate with. I left soon after arriving, feeling uncomfortable and believing they didn't care about me. I returned to my room and lay in bed listening to Barbara Streisand's A Star is Born on a portable radio cassette player. I felt sad and alone and didn't understand why I couldn't celebrate moments like others could. It is the avoidant attachment.

As a radio broadcaster, I felt at ease in a studio, speaking into a microphone — the first time I addressed a Rotary Club, I was paralysed with fear. My hands shook so much I couldn't hold my notes, and my stomach churned with nausea. This experience highlighted my fear of unfamiliar settings and the potential for critical judgment. The anxious attachment style is about our fears and anticipating potential threats.

I also recall experiencing this during my childhood in Africa when my parents befriended a Boer family. The two boys in that family, older than me by a few years, delighted in pulling down people's pants in public. One day, they targeted me at a park. To my dismay, my parents joined in the laughter instead of intervening. I felt humiliated and shocked. In response, I fled into the bush and refused to emerge until dark despite the dangers. The overwhelming sense of being ridiculed and the belief that no one cared eclipsed my fear. I wanted to punish them for failing to protect me.

We've discussed the many traumas that afflict us, but we can heal. It takes recognition and a decision to begin healing.

Healing Exercise: Being Present

It's essential to be consistent with our healing practices. Regular self-care can reduce our anxiety and self-criticism. It can be challenging to stop anxieties once they start. When I feel these anxieties building, I place my right hand on my chest and breathe deeply, saying, 'Everything is okay. Don't worry.' It is a simple way of maintaining your emotional balance when stressed. The following exercise will build awareness and self-compassion. I recommend undertaking daily for the best results.

1. *Close your eyes and take slow, deep breaths — in through your nose and out through your mouth — counting four seconds in and four seconds out.*

2. *Do this for two minutes.*

3. *Locate any anxious feelings in your body.*

4. *You might feel them as a knot in your stomach or tightness in your chest.*

5. *Place a hand gently on the area where you feel discomfort.*

6. *As you continue to breathe, send warm, compassionate energy to any area where you feel discomfort.*

7. *Don't push the feelings away; breathe into them.*

8. *Notice if the feeling shifts or eases.*

9. *When ready, take a deep breath, open your eyes, and re-centre yourself.*

I also recommend journaling when you feel anxiety so that you can recognise it before it overwhelms you. Guided meditations will also assist. I have several available to support your healing journey. Healing takes time, but building more emotional security and fulfilling relationships is possible with effort and proper support.

A new conflict challenges the progress I've made. In the next chapter, an unforeseen outcome forces me to confront a resilience I never knew existed. Am I genuinely resilient? Perhaps healing isn't just about healing but also about learning to live with who we are. How does this help as an adult?

Chapter Fifteen

Brave Heart

There's tension in the house. You feel it, sitting with Terry on the veranda. It swirls around, unsettling you.

'I'm gonna leave,' says Terry.

'Why?'

Hanging his head, in a quiet voice, 'I don't... I can't stay.'

'You're going back to them, the Sharpies, aren't you?' He continues to stare at the ground. 'Shit, you'll end up...'

Des walks out of the front door, squaring his shoulders, his face twisting into a sneer. 'What are you two bastards up to?'

You've learnt the lessons of hiding to make sure you're not noticed, not speaking up. It's your survival technique, one well-honed from previous experiences. But tonight is not one of those times. 'Fuck off.'

His eyes glitter, an unexplainable hate in them. He curls his hand into a fist. 'You wanna go, do ya?'

Getting to your feet, shouting, 'Fuck you.'

'You haven't got the guts. You're chicken.'

Terry grabs your arm, mumbling, 'Leave it. Remember Betty's rules?'

Shaking his hand off, a white-hot rage in your gut, 'He's been pushing me ever since I got here.'

Des strides into the front garden, you follow, your anger years in the making. Raising your hands, you throw a wild haymaker, stumbling, off balance.

His face lights up, and his fist strikes you on the chin.

Dazed, staggering backwards, your jaw stings. Shaking your head, you square up again and throw another punch, missing once more.

A roaring like a steam-train furnace stops you in your tracks as you're yanked backwards by the collar. Steve shouts in your face, 'What the bleedin' hell do you think you two are doing? Betty will give you both a hiding if she finds out, eh?'

Des mutters, 'He started it.'

You ball your fists, the heat in your chest still raging. 'C'mon, I'm not scared of you.'

Des snorts, 'I'll beat the shit out of you anywhere.'

Steve yells, 'Stop it.' Grips you both by the wrist, drawing you in close, menthol and beer on his breath. In a low voice, 'If you two wanna fight, I'll arrange it, but not here, not in front of the house. Bugger me.' Shaking his head, he lets go and starts walking back into the house. Pausing, over his shoulder, 'No more fighting, and get bloody well cleaned up.'

'There's blood on your chin,' Terry whispers as you push past him.

It doesn't take long for Steve to arrange the fight at a Police Boys Club in Marrickville. The officer who runs it, a friend of his, agrees that we can settle our differences in his boxing ring. Betty tut-tuts and shakes her head in disagreement when she finds out, but Steve silences her with a sharp look.

Standing in front of the low, square, brick building, an orange glow on the brickwork in the dying sunlight, mixed emotions swirl in you. Desperately wanting to teach Des a lesson, but knowing you're not good enough to beat him. Your fear is overcome by the anger still simmering below the surface.

The thump of a ball reverberates through the open door, along with shouts and laughter from those inside. Entering behind Des, noting the worn floor, from the tread of countless feet, a shiver runs down your back, seeing the boxing ring, its ropes sag to the buckled canvas.

I won't run from him.

A man in uniform approaches, shakes Steve's hand, and introduces himself as Sergeant Doyle. 'These the lads?' Steve nods. The officer's florid face cracks into a broad smile; at least someone is enjoying themselves.

His Irish brogue is music to your ears, a reminder of your mother's native tongue, but it prompts another shiver, for a different reason.

Grinning, Steve says, 'Both reckon they can fight.'

'Grand. We'll see about that.' He laughs, a deep, throaty sound from within his ample belly. The basketball players stop and stare, an expectant look on their faces; they know what's happening.

'Let's get the gear,' Sergeant Doyle says, escorting you to an old locker room. Odours of sweat and liniment fill the air.

You sneak a look at Des; his face is drawn.

Is he worried? You pump an imaginary fist. *Maybe he's not as confident as he acts.*

A pair of boxing gloves is handed to you, their surface cracked and split. 'Steve, lace him,' the sergeant says, indicating Des. 'You boyos boxed before?' taking your hands and slipping the gloves on. Shaking your head. 'Righto. These are the rules.' With a yank, he pulls the laces tight. Then, flexing the fingers on his right hand, as if making a point, he cracks one knuckle after another, rifle shots in the room. 'Listen to my instructions and stop when I say so.' With a cautionary wave, adding, 'No hitting in the bollocks. Righto. Let's crack on.'

I'm going to hit him wherever I can.

The basketballers have congregated on the benches. This is more thrilling than their usual Tuesday night, they whisper and laugh as you climb into the ring — you're sure they're making bets, and not in your favour.

Des marches to one corner, you to the opposite one. His confidence appears to have returned. *Maybe he likes an audience.* You begin to understand why the canvas floor has buckled.

The sergeant takes up his place in the centre of the ring. 'Righto, fellas, you can't fight from the corners. In the middle, and be sharpish about it.'

Hands by your side, chewing your bottom lip, you walk into the centre of the ring and wait, staring at Des. His eyes are hard; he doesn't look away. You want to, but he'll see it as weakness. Your heart races. 'Hands up,' the sergeant shouts. 'Okay, box.'

You move around the ring, reminded of the punch on the chin as you look at Des, knowing it will be over if he lands another like that. Des has a snide look in his eyes as he steps forward, throwing punch after punch at your stomach and ribs. You're protecting your head, so every one of his punches strikes its target, knocking the wind out of you. Doubled over, dropping to one knee, trying to suck in oxygen. There's a ripple of laughter from the benches.

The sergeant pushes Des back and grips your shoulder with thick, calloused fingers. 'Jesus, laddie, protect yourself,' he mutters, peering at you. 'Can you continue?'

Nodding, you gasp out a yes. Gritting your teeth, you get to your feet. All you need to do is hit him once.

He waits with an air of nonchalance, knowing he has you.

Treading warily, you move forward and lash out, hoping the punch connects. He dodges and hits you flush in the chest. Staggering, your legs bend as if made of rubber, your arms lead weights.

Des closes, his eyes signalling it's time to finish. He throws punches at your head, but in his haste, they whistle past your ear.

With relief, you hear, 'Stop. To your corners, lads.'

Staggering to the corner, Steve leans on the ropes and studies you. 'You alright? Want to keep going?' Nodding, too tired to speak. 'Right. Then, for Chrissake, hold your hands up and move around the ring, eh? You're making yourself an easy target.'

Grimacing, you want to say you're not doing it on purpose, but your mouth is busy sucking in air and it's too much effort. A hollow feeling in your stomach as the sergeant calls you back to the centre. 'One more round, lads, then shake hands. Okay?'

You exhale. *I have to survive.*

'Okay, box.'

You throw a punch. Des avoids it. He's steely-eyed as he stalks you around the ring.

Don't wait, go for him.

With a deep breath, you throw a wild roundhouse punch, catching him by surprise, it connects. He reels back, a trickle of blood from his mouth. Your heart sings at the sight; energy flowing through your veins. Des licks his lips, his tongue red, and throws a lacklustre punch. The sergeant calls a halt.

Blood streaks down Des's chin.

Back in the locker room, sinking to the bench, gasping for air, struggling to get the gloves off. The sergeant helps, squinting at you. 'I don't think boxing's your game, lad. Best go home and stay out of trouble.'

Leaving, you glance at the ring with a wry smile. It doesn't look so bad now.

Des remains silent on the way home, occasionally licking his lips.

Your chest swells with pride.

Reflections: Resilience

"I could not heal my being with my doing. To be who I am is all that matters."
— John Bradshaw

Psychiatrists describe resilience as coping with challenging events and adapting to adversity. The setbacks I experienced in Sydney took their toll. Was it desperation or resilience that kept me going? I like to think it was resilience, but it's more likely that I had no other option. The interaction with Des was a personal threat I had to deal with myself. My response was not heroic but based on fear. A fear that I would be under his control like I was with my father.

For abused children, resilience equates to survival. It is born out of fear and need for safety. It disrupts our sense of trust and self-worth, limiting our ability to fight back when faced with adversity. Our early childhood experiences can impact our ability to recognise resilience. The most common emotional responses we have indicating a lack of resilience are:

- *Frequent mood swings and anxieties.*

- *Finding it difficult to handle everyday challenges.*

- *Feeling overwhelmed in certain situations.*

- *Feeling inadequate or blaming ourselves for things that are not our fault.*

- *Exhibiting extreme shyness or aggression.*

- *Engaging in risky behaviour.*

- *Struggling at school due to difficulty concentrating.*

- *Suffering from insomnia and nightmares.*

- *Avoiding situations, people, or places that remind us of our abuse.*

Our trauma responses are intertwined with resilience. It's impossible to disentangle them as they all play a role in how we function as children and adults. As a child, my resilience came from escaping the family home and spending most of my time outdoors. Being on my own gave me a sense of safety, independence and the ability to care for myself. However, this also created a belief that I had to be solely responsible for myself as an adult.

Adult Reaction: Being Alone

It does take resilience to survive in an abusive home. It may not feel like resilience then, but we can draw on it later as a survival strength. We all have challenges in our lives from time to time. Generally, we are able to overcome them, or they don't require a great deal of resilience. But when something significant occurs, adults who've faced abuse as a child may struggle to find the necessary resilience.

My resilience was tested when I was stood down from my position with ABC Radio. It was while I was the manager of two ABC radio stations. As a new manager, I pushed myself and my team hard. My approach was demanding and unforgiving. Eventually, the staff complained, accusing me of bullying. I was suspended pending an investigation. I'll never forget the moment I walked out of the ABC office — the abrupt loss of my future, torn away by my behaviour. At home, I moped and replayed every decision I'd made for weeks. Then, something shifted. I decided to join a community group providing breakfast to underprivileged kids and found a sense of purpose again. With no word from the ABC, I decided not to wait for their decision. I applied for several jobs and got one. I walked away from the ABC without regret and found something far more valuable — a level of resilience in myself.

Many face more significant challenges than mine. Systemic sexual abuse, drugs, alcohol, gambling, sex and pornography addiction are complex areas in which finding the resilience to overcome can be difficult. And yet, we do see the strength to do so. Remember, we don't know the depth of our capabilities or resilience until tested. Let's examine how we can build resilience in our lives.

Healing Exercise: Valuing Ourselves

For some of us, life is not satisfying. We wonder why we've got a disorganised, painful, messy life. We believe we cannot have what others have: a happy home, a good job, and a stable relationship. We question whether we'd be more loveable if we were more intelligent, looked better, or had a better education. These negative thoughts impact our quality of life. However, we can achieve greater resilience and dismiss these thoughts by cultivating positive thinking, strong social connections, and implementing healthy coping strategies.

Healing is about having a supportive environment. That may be with a partner, family member, friend, or therapist. We often find ourselves stuck in behaviours that reflect our childhood trauma. When we build resilience, we develop an inner strength that helps us rebound from those behaviours.

Negative thoughts are destructive. Silence the voice in the back of your head that keeps saying you are not good enough. We need to change the narrative to a positive and affirming voice that supports us. Trust in your inner strength. You hold the power within you. To change the voice in your head, simply rephrase the negative thoughts into positive ones. 'I am good enough.' 'I will succeed.'

Volunteering with a local charity or community service organisation is another great way to develop self-belief. Also supporting a friend in need. Doing this provides a sense of purpose and self-worth. Rather than thinking we are the only ones who can do something, we learn to share and support others. It's essential to believe in ourselves. It allows us to change our thoughts and realise we're as good as others. Healing is a combination of taking care of ourselves and changing the way we think about ourselves. Confront your fears and low self-worth with this mirror technique.

1. Stand in front of a mirror.

2. Look into your eyes and say aloud, 'I am strong.' 'I am worthy of good things.'

3. Feel the connection between your words and your reflection.

4. This reinforces the truth of what you say.

5. Use this technique anytime you feel unworthy.

The most crucial growth we make is in the area of believing that we are worthy. As we begin, we may find other childhood traumas arise. Always remember, it's OK not to be OK. Take time for self-care and seek out professional help if necessary. It's not a weakness but a step toward managing your healing journey. No matter the circumstances, you will find a way out of your pain.

As I began to believe in myself, I met a girl. This challenged my inner child once again, as I became terrified of getting too close. Sharing my feelings is not something I can do. In the next chapter, we explore the issue of intimacy dysfunction, why it occurs, and how we overcome our fear of intimacy.

Chapter Sixteen

Close but Distant

The bricks fly from your hands like a discharge from a shotgun, scattering across the trailer bed. One lands on your foot. Howling, you hop from foot to foot.

Kevin leaning against the trailer, is racked by laughter, George splutters, doubled up with laughter.

Grimacing, turning away, surveying the bricks, wondering, not for the first time, why you agreed to this job.

George suggested it, at least, you think he did. At the time, he'd been devouring a ham sandwich and you weren't sure what he was saying. He put an arm around your shoulders. 'Get off, George, you stink. What were you saying about a job?'

With a cough, not an altogether healthy one to your ears, brick dust showering you as he removed his shirt. 'I told the boss about you and Kevin. For a job. He said come and see him.'

'George, we have jobs.' Kevin remained mute, which was not like him. Glancing across, his face is puckered, as if he's in pain.

What's bothering him?

George mumbled something.

'What?'

'I said, youse moan about your jobs all the time.'

With a sigh, you concede. That's true. Kevin, what do you think? You wanna give it a go?' Absently, he nods, a distant look in his eyes. 'Looks like we're gonna work with you, George.'

Beaming, slapping you on the back, he chortled, 'I knew youse would.'

You'd left the furniture factory after a few mishaps that caused Gary concern, and you wanted to get away from Sharon — she treated you like a leper. But you'd done well out of it, paying Reg back and shouting him a beer, which he appeared to appreciate more than the money. You got a job scraping solder off transistor radio circuit boards. Tedious work and an even more tedious manager. He paraded up and down between desks that were set out like a classroom, pausing every so often to watch you work. He'd rest a hand on your shoulder, leaving it there until you became uncomfortable. Your current job was mixing kitty litter in a large hopper.

'We'll have to quit, George.'

'Best wait. The boss might not go for you.' Then, as he waltzed out of the room, he added, 'We need to arrive early tomorrow,' a cheeky smile on his face.

***

Trudging along Canterbury Road at five-thirty in the morning was the first time you regretted saying yes to the job, the second, when a passing garbage truck blew exhaust fumes over you. Arriving at Canterbury Brickworks, Kevin began moaning about George jumping on top of him and forcing him out of bed that morning.

'Do we have to leave so early every morning?'

With a chuckle, George pounded him on the back. 'No. Today's special.'

Kevin, downcast, muttered, 'So what do we do at this bloody job?'

George, flexing his arms, 'You load bricks on trucks. I can pick up six in one go, and that's not easy.' That was the end of the conversation. A sleek limousine rolled up to the gate, a man in a neatly fitting grey suit and matching tie got out. George leant across and whispered, 'Make sure you tell him how much you want the job.' But you were no longer sure you did, worried about how you'd lift six bricks.

Kevin voiced your sentiment. 'Not sure we do.'

The man signalled to George. 'Are these them?' George nodded, you thought he was about to bow. 'Okay, let's get you signed up. George, get the gear they'll need.' George trotted off across the yard, past a brick building, smoke pouring from its chimney, and entered a three-sided tin shed. You and Kevin follow the boss, who waves a slip of paper at you. 'Fill this out. Payday is Friday. Days off are out of your wages. Boys, I need the trucks loaded and out every half-hour.' George returned, holding several pieces of rubber in his hands, the boss glanced at him. 'George, show them what to do, and no slacking or mucking about.'

'Yes, boss,' George said, quickly ushering us away. 'C'mon, let's get started.'

You turned the rubber bits over in your hand, then tugged on George's arm. 'What are these for?'

'Slip them over your fingers. The large piece fits into your palm. It protects your hands when you pick up the bricks, especially if they're straight out of the kiln. That's when they're bloody hot.' The more you heard about this job, the less you liked it.

Kevin tried fitting the rubber over his fist. 'Not like that, idiot,' George shouted. He slipped the rubber over Kevin's fingers, the large piece fitting snugly in Kevin's palm. 'That's how you do it.'

You stared at the empty trailer, then at the stack of bricks. There were a lot.

George began explaining what to do, but you weren't listening, the sheer number of bricks on your mind.

'Hey, did you hear me?' George snapped, tapping you on the head.

Shrugging him away, you stare at the pile of bricks again, then look at George. 'Do we have to load this many every half-hour?'

He ignored you and continued: 'The trucks drop the empty trailers, and we go to each stack and put 'em on the trailer.' He pauses, sweeping a lock of hair back from his face. 'There's an easy way to do it. Squeeze them together between your hands as you pick them up, then swing around and place them on the trailer. Okay, give it a go, Graham.' Now, foot throbbing, you have a third reason for not wanting this job.

You turn to Kevin. 'Bet you can't do it.' He can't hide his delight at your pain.

George wipes his lips with the back of his hand. 'Let me show you.' In one swift motion, he picks up six bricks, swings around and places them on the trailer. 'Push them together as you lift. Don't do too many. Four is good to start with.'

Rubbing your foot, Kevin, still smirking, 'So do it, smart-arse.' He gets four on the trailer without a problem. Muttering about the stupidity of this, you try again.

Kevin chuckles. 'Look, you made the trailer this time.'

'Fuck off.'

By the end of the day, Kevin and you are exhausted. You stumble home, head hanging, too tired to look up, arms weighing a ton, again wondering if you've made a mistake. The following day, neither Kevin nor you can move a muscle. Everything hurts. With a voice that lacks any sympathy, George says, 'You'll be okay once you get going.'

Kevin grumbling. 'I'm not sure about that.'

Two weeks later, you're both loading bricks as if you've been doing it all your life. Kevin and you begin developing arm muscles, which pleases Kevin immensely. 'This'll make girls love me,' he says, flexing one as we make our way home.

George grins, 'I reckon you need more than big arms to get a girl.' Kevin glares and lowers his arm. George continues: 'I heard Terry talking about a couple of girls he met the other day. Maybe you could learn from him. He did say one of them is interested in you, Graham.'

You do a sudden about-turn and face him. 'What? Who is? What?'

'Terry reckons you met 'em at Barn World. Says one is keen on you.'

'I don't... I...'

Kevin smiles, smacking you on the arm. 'You got a girl and you don't know it.'

'Uh, we talked to two girls at the checkout.' Unfortunately, from what you remember, neither one showed any interest in you. Still, your heart beats faster, quickening the pace, you urge Kevin and George to hurry. You want to speak with Terry.

Impatiently, you wait outside the house for him, pulse racing.

Where is he? Could George be right?

You catch a glimpse of him strolling up the street and dash towards him, shouting, 'What's this? About the girls at Barn World?'

Terry, a glint in his eye, 'Nice to see you too. Girls, what girls?'

In frustration, you grip his shoulder. 'George said, you said…'

Shaking you off, he breaks into a grin. 'Oh, them, yeah.'

'What do you mean? Oh them.'

'I've seen one of them a couple of times. Dolly. She invited us to go to the beach tomorrow. Her friend asked if you wanted to go. But you better act better than this, or you can forget it.'

You remember a girl with dark hair, but not much else. 'Are you sure?' Terry, shaking his head, walks away. Running after him, grabbing his elbow, turning him around. 'How are we gonna get there?'

He smiles. 'Dolly's got a panel van. She'll pick us up. Now fuck off and leave me alone.'

***

You wait outside like two naughty schoolboys. The past half-hour spent brushing your hair, hoping it wouldn't stick up like it tended to do, and deciding what to wear. Terry, in frustration, snapped, 'All you need is a pair of shorts. Christ, it's the beach.'

You wanted to tell him how important it was, but he turned his back and stalked out of the bathroom.

Now, leaning against the garden wall, beach towel wrapped around his waist, Terry tries to appear cool. You wonder if he really is, noticing the sweat on his forehead. You understand why he might be perspiring — sweat also rolls down your back. Sniffing under your armpit.

Do I smell?

Terry, a query on his face, 'You right?'

You still don't have a picture of the girl in your head. Nothing has surfaced other than the colour of her hair, no matter how hard you try to squeeze it out of your memory. You stop thinking about it as a van turns the corner. Or more accurately, struggles around the corner, swaying from side to side. It creaks and groans as it toils up the road like a ship in a gale. It comes to a shuddering stop across the street, exhaust pipe rattling as the engine shuts off with a bang. Terry leans across and says, 'Make sure you get along with her.'

'How can I do that? That's stupid.' But he shushes you as the girls cross the road, giggling. Your face reddens.

Terry kept telling you about Dolly's tits, so she's easy to recognise. They swing from side to side, as Terry had described them. With a yell, she scampers the last few feet and jumps into his arms. The other girl has slim, tanned legs, a pert nose and cheeks both peppered with freckles. She's wearing a yellow sundress. Straightening your shirt, hoping that your hair is behaving, you smile. No words are exchanged. Terry and Dolly separate with a wet smacking sound. Resting her head on Terry's shoulder, Dolly smiles. 'Hello, Graham, nice to meet you.' Then, with a smirk, 'Graham, this is Mary. Mary, say hello to Graham. All I've heard this week is, "Graham this and Graham that."'

Mary squeals. 'Dolly, stop it.' Shifting from foot to foot, glancing at you with a bashful smile. Mouth dry, you hang your head.

Dolly laughs. 'Oh, stop acting like school kids. C'mon, you'll both have to ride in the back.' Winking, 'And behave.' Mary squeals again.

Terry opens the rear door. 'Welcome to the shaggin' wagon.'

There's a mattress on the bed of the van floor, and a poster of Mario Milano plastered on the roof. Mary throws Terry a piercing look before climbing in. Noticing your glance at the poster, 'Dolly loves wrestling. Mario's her favourite.'

Terry slides in the front alongside Dolly, kissing her on the cheek. The back of her neck flushes red. Over her shoulder says, 'We're going to Wollongong, so get comfortable.'

Mary wraps her fingers around yours. The noise of the engine and the banging exhaust make it impossible to talk, but you don't mind, content to take a quick look at her from time to time, making sure this is real.

Dolly slows the van, turning off the main road onto a sandy track, a glimpse of golden dunes and turquoise sea through the windscreen. Rushes scrape the sides as you bump and bounce along the track, before Dolly stops the van in an empty car park. With a grin, looking across at Terry, 'It's always deserted here. C'mon, the last one is chicken.' Tittering, she hops out and removes her blouse and shorts, a red and white striped bikini underneath. Then, with a wriggle of her breasts, races away, puffs of sand follow, thrown up by her feet. Squealing, she runs into the sea and is swamped by a large wave.

Terry rips off his jeans and T-shirt, grabs a towel and goes in hot pursuit.

Mary pulls off her dress, revealing a black bikini and a cute pot belly. A coy smile crosses her face at your stare.

You don't have swimmers; your pair of old work shorts will have to do. Dropping your T-shirt, you walk hand in hand with Mary to the water, savouring the sensation of the warm sand between your toes.

Dolly is splashing about like a baby seal. 'C'mon, hurry up.' Terry grabs her around the waist and dunks her under a wave. She erupts from the water, spluttering, water streaming off her naked breasts. Arms across her chest, she screams, 'Terry. My top. Oh my god!'

He laughs. 'C'mon, show us, don't be shy.'

With a sly smile, she drops her hands. 'There, seen enough? Now find my top.'

Scrabbling around on hands and knees in the surf, buffeted by the waves, you catch bits of slimy seaweed. Terry stands and shouts, 'Got it,' waving the bikini top above his head. 'But if you want it, you gotta come and get it.' He races out of the water and up into the dunes, looking back over his shoulder, laughing. Dolly, close to tears, sits. Mary stares after Terry, lips pursed, a flash of anger in her eyes.

Sighing, knowing this might ruin your chances with Mary, you mutter, 'I'll go get it.' She glances at you with a grateful smile. There's a surge in your chest; this may mean she likes you.

Catching up to Terry, 'You're being a prick. Give it back.'

'Rack off. I'll give it back when I'm ready.'

You rip it out of his hands. 'I'll take it back.'

'Can't anyone take a bloody joke?'

'It's not a joke to her.'

'I've fucked her you know.'

'Bullshit.'

'Why do you think there's a mattress in the van?'

'Does Mary know?'

Kicking at the sand. 'How would I know? I wanna do it again. So, if she wants to stop on the way back, youse betta disappear.'

You consider what he said.

If Dolly did, then maybe... 'How are we gonna disappear?'

He says nothing more as we return to the girls. You hand Dolly her top and Terry, with a sheepish grin, kisses her.

The rest of the afternoon is spent lazing in the sun, spoiled only by Terry insisting Mary remove her top, complaining that everyone has seen Dolly's tits and we should see hers.

Annoyed, Dolly snaps, 'Stop it. Unless you prefer her to me?'

'No, never.' He wraps an arm around her waist, nibbles her neck.

She whimpers. Then, disentangling herself, she stands, brushing sand from her legs, and winks at Terry. 'Let's go for a drive.'

You and Mary are back in the rear, providing another opportunity to hold hands. After the day's events, you feel game enough to put an arm around her shoulders, and she snuggles into your chest.

You pull up on a small bluff. Dolly, with a sideways glance at Terry, innocently says, 'Would you like to go for a walk?' Before he can answer, she eyes us in the rear-view mirror. 'You two will be okay, won't you?' We both nod, happy to see them leave.

'They've done it, you know,' Mary says, as she watches them walk away, arms around each other's waists.

Pretending you don't understand, 'Done it. What do you mean?'

'You know,' she says, placing a hand on your leg. 'Do you like me?'

Trembling at the touch of her hand, you want to shout yes, but your mouth refuses to work properly, instead, you stutter, 'I, I'm ah, I...'

'You don't sound like you do.'

'I'm, I do.' Hanging your head, whispering, 'I'm not good with girls.' This is not going the way you pictured. To convince her, you repeat, 'I, I do like you.'

There's a cautious look on her face as she reaches behind her back, undoing her bikini top, letting it fall into her lap. You hold your breath, unable to believe what's happening. Your eyes fix on her breasts, covered in the same freckles as her face. They jiggle as she leans forward, placing a hand on your chest, pushing you onto your back. Her lips meet yours, and her tongue explores inside your mouth. There's swelling in your pants. Hesitantly, you touch one breast, enjoying its softness, squeezing her nipple. She hisses, taking hold of your head and guiding it onto her breast. You can taste salt. She strokes the swelling in your pants, tightening her grip and you arch in pleasure. Sliding a hand between her legs, she moans and writhes. Then, with a sudden jerk, pulls back and sobs, 'I can't.' Reaching for her top, holding it against her chest, she opens the van door and runs in the direction of Dolly and Terry.

Stunned, a hollow feeling in your stomach.

What did I do?

Sighing, the sudden rejection is a knife to your heart. Mary running away reminds you of the lack of love you've been shown your entire life.

Dolly, eyes blazing, comes running back to the van. 'What happened? Mary is crying her eyes out. What did you do?'

You raise your hands, shaking your head. 'I, we, we, uh, she got upset.'

Dolly calms. 'Her old boyfriend came back last night. I think she's scared. Because she likes you.'

'Scared? Why? Should I talk to her?'

Dolly shakes her head. 'No. Not now. I will, later.'

Terry returns, Mary trailing behind him, sniffing, wiping a hand across her nose, her cheeks tear-stained. 'Sorry. I, I...' She can't finish.

'Time to go,' says Terry, sitting in the back with you. Mary is up front with Dolly.

Standing on the pavement, watching the van roar away, you shake your head. It's the last time you expect to see her.

Girls.

Reflection: Intimacy

"As a child, I felt myself to be alone, and I am still, because I know things and must hint at things which others, as a parent, know nothing of, and, for the most part, do not want to know." — Carl Gustav

Intimacy takes many forms, but in its essence, it's a connection with others. In the face of rejection by Mary, I felt confused and worthless. What had I done to cause such a reaction? Why didn't she want me? The wounded inner child is selfish, as all children are. It only cares about its own needs and desires. I couldn't understand the rejection and became sad and angry. A reaction to protect myself from further rejection.

Our intimacy problems stem from our childhood experiences. We're not able to cope with the abandonment or rejection from our caregivers. It impacts our very being as we believe we're not worthy, and therefore no one can love us. Relationship identity comes from the modelling we observed as children. It's what we know and what we can cope with. However, when that modelling is flawed, we lose all perspective on what is right and wrong when it comes to intimacy and healthy relationships.

If we've suffered childhood sexual abuse, then we're likely to have a significantly altered view of intimacy. We may fear sex, and this can drive us to engage in excessive sexual behaviour (Hypersexuality). It's our way of trying to relieve the fear. Thinking that the more sex we have, the less likely we'll be fearful. Of course, this is not necessarily true.

We can also re-enact our trauma by either becoming involved in an abusive relationship or by attempting to control all of our relationships. It is about trying to regain the power we lost as children. We can heal from intimacy dysfunction, but first, we need to understand what is going on. Perhaps some of the following reactions feel familiar in your relationships:

- *Struggling to express your needs.*
- *Feeling disappointed in your relationships.*
- *Looking for the perfect lover.*
- *Refusing to speak to your partner when upset or angry.*
- *Distrusting your partner.*
- *Looking for reasons to sabotage the relationship.*
- *Finding it difficult to hug and caress.*
- *Feeling as if you don't belong in the relationship.*
- *Addiction to sex or pornography?*

Switching between each emotional response in one relationship is also not uncommon. That must drive our partners crazy. Our abuse also left us with a fear of people seeing the real us. So, we developed a false persona and wore a mask in our relationships. We won't openly and honestly express ourselves. It protects us from being hurt.

Adult Reaction: Perfection

As adults with intimacy issues, we seek the perfect relationship, but it's unrealistic; there is no such thing. We chase a perfect, all-consuming love, and when we meet someone and realise they can't provide it, we look for flaws as a pretext to end the relationship. For years, when I began a new relationship, I already began planning an exit strategy. Then, when it does end, as it will, I tell myself I was right; they weren't for me and repeat the cycle.

I also struggled to be faithful in my relationships; I wanted someone to give me what I needed: love and care. It didn't matter how many relationships I had. I was never satisfied. There was an emptiness that needed more. When I told my wife that I no longer belonged in the marriage, it was the fear of abandonment and loss that led me to feel insecure within the marriage. Looking at my other relationships, I understand that I never genuinely connected in any of them. I kept a space between them and me. Now that I know about my wounding, I see how it's influenced my adult behaviour. I have lived with the fear of intimacy for so long that sometimes it feels like a safe blanket. But we must heal our intimacy dysfunctions and allow ourselves to have healthy and fulfilling relationships.

Healing Exercise: Nurturing

We must first reflect on our relationships to understand how we can heal. List all past relationships and how they developed or failed. See if the same problems keep repeating. If there's a pattern — and I imagine there will be — then be honest and commit to changing the behaviour. Change comes slowly, but unless you try, change will never happen. Healing intimacy dysfunction is about learning to take care of yourself first to benefit you and your relationships. The following exercise will help nurture you. To begin, place a hand on any part of your body.

1. *Stroke your skin gently.*

2. *As your hand glides along your body, feel the comforting sensations.*

3. *During this process, keep reminding yourself that you deserve kindness.*

4. *Repeat as often as is necessary.*

Other ways to assist the healing process include finding an organisation or community group willing to talk about intimacy. It may not be easy at first, but it won't take long before you can share what happened to you. It's essential to keep in mind that these are survivors, too. You can learn how to join my group in the book's resource pages.

When I began speaking about my childhood trauma, I felt a weight lift from my shoulders. I now find it liberating to share my story when asked. I'm also amazed at how many people have suffered or know someone who's suffered childhood abuse. We must take responsibility for our actions and our relationships. I contacted former lovers to apologise for my behaviour. Not all of them welcomed my apology, but this was as much for me as it was for them. Seek out a professional therapist who works with abused children in the area of intimacy dysfunction for more help on your healing path. We must break unhealthy patterns and create new ones to have healthy relationships. What happened to us was not our fault.

Mary's rejection stripped me of my sense of worthiness. More concerning, it set me on a familiar path of self-destruction, as I sought to distract myself from the pain. But the instinct to run from violence was no longer there; I welcomed the inevitable. Is this a sign of strength or a failure? The next chapter will explore how we confront and overcome our self-destructive side.

Chapter Seventeen

Facing the Abyss

Weeks pass, and no word from Mary. You've ventured to Barn World hoping to see her, but no luck.

Terry continued to see Dolly but ignored you when asking about Mary.

Sitting on the veranda, not knowing what to do, with no point asking Terry. You hear the front door open, loud voices from Alfie and George as Kevin steps out, a slice of toast in hand. 'Betty's closing up, if you want any more brekky,' stuffing toast into his mouth.

Terry is close behind. 'Hey, you wanna go to Roselands?'

Your instinct tells you it's not a good idea, but you have no idea why. Ignoring it, as Terry says there'll be lots of girls there. Pushing all doubt away, glumly agreeing.

There's nothing else to do.

Kevin pipes up, 'Great. I'll come.'

Terry nudges you, a warning glare on his face as he rolls his eyes. 'If you're coming, you're not wearing that stupid fuckin' hat.'

Kevin opens his mouth to argue, then gauges the look on Terry's face and shuts it again. 'Okay.'

'Thank Christ,' says Terry.

***

The doors hiss open, releasing a welcome blast of cold air. You've never seen a place like Roselands. Saturdays must be popular; there's a buzz of excited, chattering voices. Children, faces smeared with ice cream, clamber over plastic models of a kangaroo and emu. A carousel's red and white striped awning rotates as music plays, those on board squealing in delight.

Craning your neck upwards, staring at floor after floor of shops. Chandeliers hang from the ceiling, reflecting dazzling light throughout the building. But for you, the most amazing thing is the stairs, moving silently up and down, jammed with people.

Terry takes hold of your arm, nodding towards a fountain. Water runs down its sides into a pond surrounded by a low brick wall, but he isn't interested in the design. It's the three girls near it who have Terry's, and now your attention. They have short-cropped hair, wearing miniskirts and knitted jumpers. Terry whispers, 'I've seen them before,' with a shake of his head. 'Fuck 'em. Let's check upstairs.'

Pushing your way through the crowd, looking forward to stepping onto the moving stairs. At the top, you stop outside a men's clothing shop, mesmerised by the brightly coloured pants and shirts, hesitating, trying to picture yourself buying any of them.

A glance down reminds you of the door-to-door salesman who'd come to the house claiming he had good clothes at cheap prices. He led the way to a white van parked across the street. That may have been a clue as to their quality, but you were excited at the prospect of new clothes.

Opening the rear doors, he waved his hand at a stack of boxes filled with shirts and pants — clue number two. He suggested you could pay them off a little each week. Unable to resist, you bought a pair of corduroy flares and a striped, white and blue cheesecloth shirt. He turns up every Friday afternoon, as regular as clockwork, for his money. You're unsure of the cost, but you think you paid more than they were worth — especially after discovering Betty had suggested he come around.

Kevin wheezed, his face a pasty grey sheen, like old plasticine. Terry noticed, suggesting he sit. Kevin nodded, slumping onto a bench, placing his head between his hands.

You exchange a worried glance with Terry, and you're about to suggest going home when he nudges you. 'It's them.'

'Who?'

'The girls from downstairs.' You take greater interest now and study them closely.

Kevin raises his head. 'Girls. What girls?'

Terry ignores him, 'Let's see if they follow. You okay, Kevin?' He nods, still looking around for the girls.

They're standing near the stairs, heads close together whispering to each other. One glances up and smiles at Kevin. He moves in, says something, and you watch in dismay as the girl's back stiffens, and they stalk off.

Terry, face reddening, growls, 'What did you say to them? You've pissed them off.'

'Fuck off. I only said hello.'

Furious, he barks, 'Let's go to the fountain. If they turn up, keep your mouth shut, Kevin.'

They're not at the fountain, not that you expected them to be — you figure they've gone home. Terry shrugs. 'Let's wait. Maybe they'll turn up. If they do...' He left the sentence unfinished as he glared at Kevin.

Kevin ignored him, wheezed. 'How long are we gunna stay?'

Terry shoots him a withering stare, muttering under his breath. Then you hear a sharp intake of breath. Hoping it's the girls, you spin your head around, but unable to see them, you turn back to Terry.

'What is it? What's up?'

His face pale, he lifts his chin to indicate something above. Looking up, your blood runs cold. Lining the railing, eyes fixed on the three of you, are Sharpies, a lot of them. And the three girls are with them.

'Fuckin' hell. Sharpies,' Terry says in a low voice. 'This is trouble, I...' He doesn't finish as five march down the stairs and form a semicircle in front of you. A skinny boy with a pock marked face, steps toward you with a look he might reserve for finding something distasteful on the bottom of his shoe. The other four stare, eyes as hard as flint.

Heart pounding, sweat trickles down your back. Terry is silent. Kevin chews on his lower lip. The semicircle tightens as the pockmarked boy leans in. 'You cunts tried to pick up our girls?' A flicker of disgust in his eyes as he focuses on Terry.

'Wadda you doin' with these long hair shits?'

Terry, shaking his head. 'We weren't doing nuthin.'

You sneak a look at Kevin, then whisper in his ear. Pock mark snarls, 'What are you whispering about, prick?'

You nod towards Kevin. 'He's not well. Let him go, we'll stay.' Terry moves towards you as if to say something, but with a slight shake of your head, you stop him.

Why am I sticking my neck out?

A calmness comes over you. This is not like last time. There's no fear. You look at the Sharpies and smile to yourself.

They're scared too.

Cunning eyes look at you, then at Kevin, then back at you.

'Alright. He can fuck off. But you two aren't going anywhere.' Watching Kevin go, your heart sinks.

Terry repeats, 'We didn't do anything.'

'You wanted to fuck us,' one of the girls yells out, the Sharpies burst into snide laughter.

Another shouts, 'Dogs.'

'Is that right? Did you wanna fuck 'em?' He knows you're at his mercy. Shaking your head, 'No.'

Sensing something is about to happen, the other four lower their arms. 'Come outside,' he snarls. 'Or youse chicken?'

The centre is beginning to empty; nobody takes any notice of you or the boys surrounding you. *You betta hurry Kevin.*

'Against all of you? I don't...'

He cuts you off. 'Chickenshits. Tell you what. If you can beat one of us, we'll let you go.' You remember Campsie. They'd never let you walk away. Sweat rolls down his face. He lowers his voice. 'Youse think you're better than us. Don't you?'

A yell from above, startles everyone.

What now?

You look up in disbelief as another boy makes his way hurriedly down the stairs. 'Shit, is that Terry?' A weak smile crosses Terry's face as his hand is pumped up and down. 'I haven't seen you in ages. What've you been up to?'

Terry grins. 'Craig. How are you?'

Craig turn s to the others, the five are joined by more Sharpies as they swarm down the stairs like locusts, all surprised at this turn of events.

You're dumbfounded, not sure what's happening.

'I met Terry when I was with the Town Hall lot.' Craig pauses, smiling. 'We rolled this old pisshead. Terry got caught. Never dobbed on us.' The tension evaporates as they move in to shake Terry's hand and slap him on the back. Pock mark is not happy, his lips part in a snarl, realising his chance to beat the shit out of you is slipping away.

The girls feel the same. 'What about us?'

Craig yells, 'Shut up.' Taking Terry's arm, 'You wanna come with us?' Winking and nodding at the girls.

Terry shakes his head. 'No. I'd better get going.'

'If you change your mind, you're welcome. It'll be like old times.' In a quiet voice, he mutters, 'Don't bring the others.'

As you walk away, pockmark slinks alongside. 'Youse are lucky,' he rasps, 'We had others outside waiting to kick your fuckin' heads in.'

You imagine he'd be in his element watching, laughing and sinking a boot in as you lay on the ground.

The doors suck closed. Shaking, not only in fear but also anger, until George, Kevin and Neal come running across the car park. Neal shouts, 'You okay?' His face flushed, ready for a fight.

'Yeah. Terry knew one of them. But thanks for coming.'

Terry sniggers, 'Was that what you said to Kevin?'

You nod.

Neal claps you on the back. 'Gotta take care of each other.'

Words you've heard before.

***

It happened when the police turned up at the house a week ago — not an unusual event. Kevin, Terry and you stay out of the way until they leave. Betty was in the kitchen, leaning against the sink, eyes red from crying.

Kevin was the first to speak. 'What's wrong?'

'Peter's in hospital. They don't think he'll live.'

Shocked, we all spoke at once. 'What? How?'

She sobbed. 'He was beaten up on his way home.' Tears, fat and heavy, roll down her cheeks, plopping onto the linoleum floor. Neal, hearing the commotion, joins us. Betty wipes a hand across her face. 'I'm going to bed. You boys get your own dinner.'

As she left, Neal, in a gruff voice, said, 'We gotta take care of each other.' You didn't know what he was thinking, but were wary.

Terry said, 'I bet it's the Campsie Sharpies. They're real pricks.'

You didn't need to be reminded of them; the incident in the park was still vivid in your memory. Terry continued, 'I can get a car.'

Neal nodded. 'Alright, do that.' Adding, 'Not a word to Betty.'

Terry arrived with a four-door Corolla. He didn't say where or how he'd got it. Neal, carrying a baseball bat, slid into the front seat, the bat disappearing underneath. 'Let's go,' he said. Neal stopped one boy on a pushbike who was so scared of him and the bat that he wet his pants. Neal let him go. Peter died the next day. His family requested that none of us attend the funeral.

Reflection: Self-Destruction

"What a child doesn't receive, he can seldom later give." — P.D. James

Due to our abuse, we can exhibit signs of self-destruction early in life. However, they are usually unrecognised as genuine trauma responses. As children, they may appear as being lazy or disinterested. The self-destruction wound develops from the belief that we're no good. For example, I ignored my inner caution about not going to the shopping centre, as my only thought was: I didn't care what happened to me because no one else did.

Children, when told something often enough, come to believe it, and so it is with the belief that we are not worthy. Self-destruction symptoms can manifest at any time and may look like the following:

- *Avoiding opportunities for growth, success or happiness.*

- *Deliberately failing in school.*

- *Engaging in self-harm to cope with emotional pain.*

- *Undertaking reckless actions to punish ourselves.*

- *Pushing away people who care about us out of fear of rejection.*

- *Feeling we don't deserve love leads to loneliness.*

- *Repeating relationship cycles that mirror our childhood.*

- *Seeking out abusive or emotionally unavailable people.*

- *Constantly blaming ourselves for not being good enough.*

- *Engaging in perfectionism that leads to burnout and self-loathing.*

We also seek self-destruction in addictive behaviour with drugs, alcohol, food, gambling or sex to fill the emptiness. These addictions make us feel good and numb the pain. No matter how fleeting that numbing is.

According to the US National Centre for Health Statistics, between 2001 and 2021, the most significant increase in suicide rates for men occurred among those aged fifty-five to sixty-four, a twenty-five per cent increase. And a forty-four per cent increase for women in the sixty-five to seventy-four age group. It's impossible to know if this is a result of childhood trauma, as there are likely to be other factors. However, I believe the wounded inner child has played its part.

Adult Reaction: Hopelessness

The feeling that we don't belong in this world can increase as adults. We think we should be able to cope like everyone else but struggle to overcome our challenges because of our feelings of being worthless. We've been in the dark about the damage to our inner child for years. I accepted the beatings I received as a child, believing I deserved whatever happened. As an adult, I realised I was in trouble when I felt a sadness like a black shroud falling over me. I couldn't see my way out. I tried suicide and didn't like it. While staying at the People's Palace, I made my first attempt.

A more focused effort occurred while driving on a country road. I didn't feel particularly sad that day, but I experienced a sudden feeling of hopelessness. I had a strong urge to drive the car off the road and into a tree; I fought with the steering wheel to stop from leaving the road. My inner voice said, 'No one cares, do it.' I regained my senses by thinking about my children. I'm not sure anything else would've stopped me. I mention this because that's how quickly our moods and feelings can change. We get up in the morning feeling great, and then, out of the blue, we feel down, sad, and worthless. I have at times stood on a beach looking out to the ocean, thinking, would anyone notice if I slipped away?

The negative inner voice is one of the most corrosive things that happens to us. We struggle to stop it. 'We'll never amount to anything,' or 'We're not as good as others.' And my favourite, 'You'll never succeed.' The negative voice chips away at our confidence and self-esteem. It leaves us with a belief that no one cares. Because we don't understand what is happening to us, we become aggressive and destructively re-enact our trauma through dangerous actions. We need to take time to understand ourselves and recognise when we're in trouble. If we want to heal, we must commit to doing the work. If we don't, we won't stop the self-destructive feelings.

Healing Exercise: Acceptance

Like all poor behaviour, we must address it to change it. Let's begin by tackling the negative voices in our heads. They come from our trauma and the fears that the trauma has created. Consider what the negative voice in your head is saying. Is it telling you that 'You're not good enough?' or 'That you're unworthy of love?' These are manifestations of the wounded inner child. This voice doesn't like to be silenced and will fight back if you try to stop it. But as long as you commit to the healing work, you'll be successful.

Let's begin by giving our negative voice a name. Mine is Edgar. You want an unusual name to avoid confusion with someone you may know. When Edgar starts speaking, I raise my hand and say, 'Edgar, Stop. I'm not listening to you.' It doesn't take long for Edgar to diminish; the more you say it, the less it will appear. Mine has completely gone. Be consistent and be firm. We must dismiss all thoughts that we're not good enough. We are and can show the world that we are.

Another tool for understanding ourselves is writing down our thoughts and experiences. Write ten things you don't like about yourself. Then, write ten things you like about yourself. Consider the things you don't like and commit to stopping them. Look at the things you want and try to live by them. Make it a daily ritual to repeat the ten things you like.

We should recognise how far we've come on our healing journey and how much inner strength we have. The following exercise will also help you improve your self-belief:

1. Place your hand on your heart and say, 'I acknowledge myself.'

2. *Repeat this, getting louder and louder.*

3. *Feel the emotions in your body.*

4. *Don't push them away.*

5. *Embrace the fact that you're here and are moving forward.*

6. *Use this acknowledgement of your inner strength each day.*

We must empower ourselves and take control of our healing. All of these exercises are valuable in providing healing. It's up to each of us to choose which healing method suits us best. As always, it is vital to consider professional therapy. A step that further aids in our healing process.

I was trying to understand my self-destructive tendencies and find a way to overcome their hold on me. But when confronted with two new events, I'm thrust back into a different trauma. Attachment disorder is a condition that makes it challenging to have healthy and secure relationships or leaves us with a lack of boundaries. Next, we'll examine its impact and how we can unravel its complexities.

Chapter Eighteen

Lost Connection

When Alfie swears at Kevin over a Weet-bix, you know all isn't right in the house.

The argument is so heated that Betty intervenes, tearing the Weet-bix in half, throwing the pieces into their respective bowls, shouting, 'There, now bloody eat it.' Alfie mutters and stomps off to his bedroom, slamming the door, leaving his half untouched. Kevin eats both.

As you leave the dining room, a thong flies past your ear, bouncing off the wall.

Turning around, Terry's behind you, 'What the hell?' He mutters, 'I hate spiders.' The spider in question has scuttled away, unharmed.

'What's wrong with you? You've been shitty all week.'

Distracted, fiddling with his shorts, something is obviously on his mind. He exhales, resignation in his voice. 'I'm leaving.'

You've heard it before. In fact, you've said it at one time or another.

'Betty says if I go, she won't take me back.' He stops, stares into the distance, a mournful look on his face. 'She reckons I'll do something stupid.'

'She's probably right. Where will you go?'

Terry grimaces. 'Yeah, s'pose I'd like to go see me mum, see how she is. It's also bloody Dolly. She wants to be with me all the time. Dead set accuses me of being with someone else when I'm not.' Pausing, picking up his thong, slipping it on, 'Fuckin' sheilas.'

You haven't seen Terry since that last conversation. One morning during breakfast, he wanders in as if he'd never left.

You stare. 'Where've you…?'

Interrupting, he smirks, 'With Dolly.' There's a silly grin on his face as he reaches for the Froot Loops box, shaking it, moaning, 'It's empty.' Looking around. 'Anymore?'

'Did you see your mum?'

With a shake of his head, 'Nah, she wasn't home. I didn't hang around in case the old prick caught me. Bastard would've called the police, like last time. So, I went and met up with Dolly.'

'So you're back with her. You said she pissed you off.'

He leans across the table. 'Yeah, she does, but…' Terry shakes the box again. 'Bloody hell, I'm hungry.'

'But what?' He scoffs, changing the subject. 'I got news. Mary broke up with her boyfriend.'

Biting your lip, your heart pounds, 'Did she? Is she?'

'Dolly reckons they got into a big fight about her dad. Anyway, you're not interested. Are you?'

'Um, if she…'

Terry smacks his palm against his forehead. 'Course you're not. Want me to find out if she's interested in seeing you?'

Do I?

You were hurt last time, but the feeling of her in your arms, the tang of salt on her breasts. Sighing, 'I guess so?'

Your pulse races as, blushing, you concentrate on your cereal.

Terry exclaims, 'For fuck's sake,' stomping off into the kitchen.

***

Dolly is perched on the bonnet of her van, watching as you and Terry approach. Uncrossing her legs, sliding to the ground, she straightens her skirt and then wraps her arms around him. Over his shoulder, she winks. 'Hi Graham. You looking for Mary? Hoping she'll burst out of the back?' snorting, 'We'll go get her from her place,' laughing at the look of disappointment on your face.

Mary is skittish like a newborn pony, constantly looking back at her house, then quickly back at the street as the van stuttered to a halt.

You fling the door open and race over, a familiar hollowness in your stomach.

She steps back, placing a hand on your chest. 'Quick, let's go...'

Pushing past you, squeezing into the front seat.

Deflated, climbing into the rear, noticing that the Rolling Stones have replaced Mario Milano.

The van vibrates and shudders as it takes off. 'I know a place,' Dolly shouts. 'Not many people go there.' The rattling and banging from the engine drowns out any further chance of conversation. Dolly turns onto a rough dirt track, stopping at a grassy clearing. A chain-link fence and padlocked gate block further progress. A sign reads, NO ENTRY. Sewage Plant. It's clear why the area isn't popular.

Dolly grins. 'It's quiet, if you don't mind the smell.'

Mary twirls a strand of hair between her fingers, looking at you with a shy smile. 'We can stay in the van.' Turning away, her face reddening.

Dolly prods Terry. 'They want to talk.' She winks. Terry and she walk away, disappearing behind a clump of trees.

Mary climbs into the rear, one eyebrow raised. 'You still upset with me?'

'Um... no.' You're picturing her freckle-covered breasts.

'You know I broke up with my boyfriend.'

'Uh, oh, yes, Terry told me. Sorry.'

'Nah, don't be. I only went with him to spite my dad.'

Her fingers run up your forearm.

Your breathing constricts. With a gulp, you try to concentrate on what she's saying, but your mind is racing.

She leans forward, kissing your cheek.

You fumble with her buttons, frustrated, unable to get the last one undone. She titters, undoing it. Without hesitation, you slip your hand inside her shirt and over a breast, cupping it.

She moans, gasping, 'Take 'em off.'

Fingers shake as you unzip. She slides her panties off, flicking them across the van.

Leaning towards you, her tongue runs down the side of your neck, and then, with a wicked glint in her eye, she climbs on top, guiding you inside.

Unable to control yourself, you cry out at each thrust. A tingle races up your legs and backbone until it feels like it will burst out the top of your head.

Mary wails.

Stopping, fearing you've hurt her, she hisses, 'Don't stop.'

You push harder, and then, with a moan and a shudder, flow into her.

Lying arm in arm, soaking up a moment, neither of you wants to end until Mary breaks the silence. 'We should get dressed.'

'No. I like lying here like this.'

She giggles. 'I know what you like.'

There's a holler from Dolly. Followed by a thump on the side of the van. 'Hey, you two ready to go?'

Collapsing into fits of laughter, Mary wipes a tear from her eye, shouting back, 'Yes.' Clutching her panties in one hand, she glances at you. 'Do you wanna...?' Before she can finish speaking, the van door opens and Terry and Dolly are there, grinning.

'You two finished talking?' There's an innocent smile on Dolly's face. 'If so, we should get going.'

You hold Mary in your arms on the way home, kissing her on the lips as she hops out. 'See you soon,' she says, waving goodbye.

***

As you and Terry walk down the driveway, stars emerge, twinkling and sparkling, mirroring your heart.

Pushing the front door open, it jams against a duffel bag.

Stepping over the bag, you hear Betty's voice, loud and rough, echoing in the hallway. You've never heard her like this.

Exchanging a glance with Terry, a question in your eyes. He raises his shoulders, shaking his head.

Warily, entering the lounge room, Betty is seated, elbows resting on the table. 'You're home. Good. Sit down.'

Terry and you pull out chairs.

'Yes, there, anywhere.' Her face is as hard as stone.

What's going on?

George and Kevin are sitting on one side of the table, their heads bowed, Alfie and Des sit opposite. Neal is at the far end, face pale, his red-rimmed eyes look at you, then he drops his head, his forearms tremble.

Betty, in a low voice that carries clearly across the room, 'Neal's leaving. He... he's...'

Alfie pipes up. 'Leaving. Leaving. No. No. No leaving.'

Betty chops her hand down onto the table. 'Quiet, Alfie. You're not leaving.' Alfie slinks down in his chair, hurt in his eyes. Neal continues to stare at the table, his fingers picking at a hole in the plastic cover.

Terry looks at Betty, then at Neal. 'What's going on?'

Betty, white spittle on her lips, snaps, 'You want to tell them or shall I?'

You shrink in your seat, not understanding what's happening, but the hate in her voice triggers deep fears in you. It's your father again.

Neal remains silent.

'Well, if you're not gonna, I will.' Taking a deep breath, she spits out the words. 'Neal's a poofter. I found a boy in his room last night.'

The words are like a hammer blow.

I knew I'd seen something that night.

Betty's fury is plain to see on her face, eyes blazing, breasts heaving under her faded housecoat. She screeches, 'This won't be allowed under my roof!' Slamming her palm on the table.

Terrified, shaking, you stare at a tomato-sauce stain, avoiding eye contact.

Shoving her chair back, she marches out of the room.

Stunned, you cower, not raising your eyes or uttering a word in Neal's defence. He whispers to himself, then the clatter of his chair.

Wanting to shout that he should stay, instead, you remain silent. The front door *clicks* as it closes. Shame washes over you, you're a coward — the self-belief that had begun disappears, swallowed up by fear. Your heart breaks for Neal and for you.

Reflection: Attachment Disorder

"By reparenting our inner child, we can release and heal the pain from the past."
— Margaret Paul

In a previous chapter, I discussed anxious, avoidant, and disorganised attachment styles. These have a significant impact on our lives; however, they tend to be milder in reaction than attachment disorders. These are more severe and caused by extreme neglect and abuse. There are two predominant attachment disorders:

- **Reactive Attachment Disorder** *is characterised by having difficulty in forming healthy and secure relationships and managing emotional responses. With this disorder, we tend not to be positive and are irritable, sad, or fearful. We don't respond to comfort when we're upset and have difficulty making eye contact. We're not inclined to engage in physical touch such as hugging. As a child, we are disobedient and prone to arguing.*

- **Disinhibited Social Engagement Disorder** *is characterised by the lack of boundaries. As children, we aren't shy or hesitant around adults. We will be overly friendly and talkative with them. This can lead to us going somewhere with a stranger without question or hesitation and without letting any adult know. Both of these disorders originate from inconsistent caregiving, creating a deep sense of insecurity and hypervigilance.*

I've discussed how my relationship skills are poor. Much of this is due to my reactive attachment disorder. However, I also suffered from disinhibited social engagement disorder. An example of this was while living in Cape Town. I would've been eight years old and loved going to Saturday morning matinees at the cinema. I always went on my own. One day, as I left the cinema, a boy dashed into the road and was struck by a car. Everyone stood around waiting for the ambulance. A man tapped my shoulder, asking if I wanted to help by fetching a blanket for the injured boy. I agreed, happy at the thought of being able to help. The man clutched my arm as he guided me along the pavement and up the stairs to an apartment. Inside, another man was standing in the bedroom. The man who escorted me began talking about African witch doctors and how they could cast spells on people. As he spoke, a wordless exchange passed between the two men. The first man took me by the arm, forcibly walking me towards the door, telling me to leave. There was no blanket.

As a child, when someone we rely on isn't responsive, our ability to know our boundaries is impacted, both in what we should and shouldn't do within relationships.

Adult Reaction: Emotional Neglect

My view of the world changed when I reconnected with Mary. The world was a good place again. However, Neal's abrupt departure reinforced my fears of how quickly my world can change.

Attachment disorders significantly influence our approach to relationships as we have learnt to view the world as a dangerous place. If we aren't exposed to a range of emotions as a child, it isn't easy to recognise emotions in others and ourselves as adults. It also leaves us unable to express emotions like others might. We become incapable of identifying, acknowledging, or responding to our own emotions or our partner's. This makes us uncomfortable with intimacy.

As an adult, we experience fear of intimacy or become emotionally unavailable. Sometimes, our distrust makes us suspicious of other people's motives and actions. We rarely ask for help or rely on others. We might even prefer not to be in a relationship.

If we are, we can act dismissively towards our partner or feel we don't need to include them. In essence, we manage two relationships within one.

My parents didn't show me love, but that doesn't mean they were always unkind. I remember moments of joy. My father took me to see the movie Goldfinger. I remember feeling grown up, safe and loved during those two hours. I was mistaken. It was not love or safety. The moments I experienced with my father were fleeting and misleading. My confusion and despair deepened because of the inconsistency in his emotional responses. Each time he changed or was emotionally unavailable, it confirmed my belief that I was unwanted. When we receive inconsistent reassurances, we never feel secure. However, an attachment disorder doesn't mean we can't make friends or have good relationships. I remember, at nineteen, working in a pathology laboratory with great friends. We used to socialise together regularly. As I look back, I realise I never truly felt like I fit in — even then. A voice inside my head always whispered that I didn't belong. I had similar experiences working in nightclubs in Darwin. The feeling of not fitting into the local social circle persisted. Even though I knew everyone, I always felt alone when at a party or social function.

Attachment disorders make us fear everything, including relationships. This results in us becoming disconnected from our relationships, particularly romantic ones, as we are incapable of truly committing for fear of being abandoned. Other attachment disorder symptoms that impact us include finding it hard to trust, being a poor communicator, struggling to talk about our feelings, wanting love but being scared by someone offering it and the inability to face conflict.

Healing Exercise: Visualisation

We must nurture our inner child to help our healing process. Start with understanding your relationships. Be open about your feelings and find ways to talk to your partner about how you feel and what stops you from giving to the relationship. Also, recognise that our inner child often feels scared and fearful. By showing it care and love, you are providing care and love for yourself. It's healthy to provide the comfort it needs while you explore what you require as an adult. The following exercise focuses on creating positive feelings. It provides an opportunity to increase self-compassion and reduce stress.

1. *Find a relaxing position and close your eyes.*

2. *Take a deep breath, in through your nose and out through your mouth.*

3. *Breathe deeply for a minute, allowing yourself to settle.*

4. *Locate any stressful feelings in your body.*

5. *Stress often shows up in the stomach or chest.*

6. *Send breaths into any part of your body that feels stressed.*

7. *Don't try to get rid of these feelings; breathe into them.*

8. *Sit quietly for a minute and notice if any part of your body softens.*

9. *Now, I want you to visualise your inner child.*

10. *If they are scared, think about how to respond to them. What will you say?*

11. *Speak slowly in a warm, friendly and reassuring voice.*

12. *Let them know you love them.*

13. *Absorb the feelings and connection with your inner child.*

14. *Let those feelings flow through your body.*

15. *Take a deep breath and open your eyes.*

We can heal attachment disorders, as they are not permanent. But healing requires self-awareness, self-care and finding healthy relationships. Working with a professional therapist who understands attachment disorders will also be of great value in your healing journey.

My world was turned upside down when Neal left. My inner child's fear of a dangerous world took hold once more. I leaned on Mary for support until an unforeseen incident fuelled my rage. In the next chapter, we'll uncover the cost of unchecked anger.

Chapter Nineteen

Unspoken Truth

Betty kicking Neal out brought back painful memories. A shudder racks your body as you recall the anger and hate in her voice. Relieved that now you have someone to talk to about how you feel. Another glance towards Barn World — still no movement.

She has to finish soon.

As you wait, you think about that morning's conversation with Terry. He was searching for something in your wardrobe. Poking his head out, 'Have you seen my sneakers?'

'They're not here.'

Grumbling, 'Shit. Where are they then?'

'You didn't mean that stuff you said... about Neal, did you?'

'Yes. How could he stay after what he did? Jeez, where are they?' Going back to his search.

'You're a shithead. What about Roselands? He came to help.'

A muffled reply about not needing him came from the cupboard. He stood and stomped out of the bedroom, muttering about hurting whoever had his sneakers — which you know are on Kevin's feet.

Mary skipped across the road.

Watching her, your heart ached. You lean in to give her a kiss, pulling back, she gasps, 'No, not here, my boss might see.'

Annoyed, pursing your lips, sulkily, 'Where then?'

Giggling, fluttering her eyelashes, 'Don't be mad. The park's quiet, and I've brought something for you.'

'Did you? What?'

'C'mon. I'll show you.'

Sneaking a sidelong glance at her, admiring her freckled, pert nose, your chest swells with delight. You find it difficult to believe she likes you.

Strolling through the park, an elderly couple silently watches, hands clasped together. A family of ducks scatter as you pass, squawking, as they scramble back to the safety of the pond.

Mary, taking your hand, leads you towards a shrub near an empty playground. 'No one will see us here.' She tugs on her skirt, wrapping it around her legs as she sits, taking a packet of Lemon Crisps out of her bag. 'Do you like these?'

'Uh, sure.'

'You expected something else?' Her face is a mirror of innocence.

Casting your eyes down, you take the offered biscuit, covering up your embarrassment. Then begin to tell her about the night's events. Tears prick at your eyes as you think of Neal. Brushing them away, 'I should've said something.'

The colour drained from her face. Averting her gaze, picking at the grass, 'I'm glad you didn't, or you...'

'I let him down.'

'If you'd said something, you might have been thrown out too. Then we...' Moving closer, sliding a hand between your legs. 'Then we couldn't do this.'

Thoughts of Neal, Betty and Terry vanish in the blink of an eye, a white-hot heat replacing them. Gasping, 'We can't, not here, I...'

Smirking, she continues to squeeze. You undo the buttons on her shirt, sliding your hand inside. She whispers in your ear, 'I missed you.' Pulling your zipper down, her hand disappears inside. Pressing your lips against hers, a tingle along your spine. Breathlessly, she murmurs, 'You want to?'

Throat tight, you nod.

The old couple are still there, but neither looks in your direction. The ducks have reappeared, continuing to feed on the grass — you don't think they'll mind.

Mary kicks off her shoes, reaches under her skirt, pulling her panties off. You catch a glimpse of black hair.

'Get them off,' she says, tugging at your pants.

Wriggling, you wrench them down over your hips. 'Shit, they won't...'

Laughing, she shoves them to your ankles. 'You look ready.'

A guttural moan from deep inside as she takes hold, placing a finger on your lips. 'Shhh.' Her breathing heavy. 'Quick, get on top.' Fumbling, unable to put yourself inside, she moans, 'Move up,' arching her back.

'I can't... it's not...'

Taking hold, she slides you inside; your mouth opens in pleasure. Her fingernails dig into your shoulders as you hang onto each other.

Mary rolls onto her side. 'I have to go. My dad will worry if I'm late.'

'You free tomorrow?'

Giggling, she simpers, 'You want more? C'mon, get up.' Brushing the leaves off her skirt, smoothing it down with a few strokes of her hand, she runs her tongue around her lips, sniggering at your expression.

Walking back through the park, now bathed in shadows, the old couple have gone. The ducks have also disappeared. For you, the world is right again.

'Where do you catch the bus?'

'Over there,' nodding at a bus shelter across the street, next to a dilapidated phone box. 'Oh hell, look, it's coming.'

Laughing in glee, you run through the park hand in hand, arriving ahead of the bus.

Brakes squeal as it comes to a stop. Mary clambers up the steps, pays the driver, takes a window seat and blows you a kiss. With a hiss of brakes, the bus moves away.

Sauntering home, you feel giddy and light-headed.

The banging of pots and pans from the kitchen sounds more enthusiastic than usual for Betty. You hear her muttering to herself. Hoping nothing else has happened, you join her in the kitchen. 'Where'd you go? I've been waiting,' she snaps.

Taken aback by her abrupt manner, 'I, um...'

'You had a visitor.'

Confused, you don't understand. 'A visitor.' You repeat. 'Who?'

'Your father.'

Her words are a meat cleaver to your heart. The colour drains from your face; there's a weakness in your legs. Shaking your head, 'No. No. He can't. No. Not here.'

Betty stares, a flicker of sympathy on her face. 'Well, he was. Standing there, where you are, not more than an hour ago.' She turns away, rummaging in a cupboard. 'Ah, found you,' pulling out a black pot. 'He wants to talk to you. He gave me... where is it?' Banging the pot onto the stove, searching in her apron pocket, 'Here,' holding up a crumpled business card.

Shaking your head, still unable to believe it. 'What? How?'

He asked you to call. There's a number on the back, I think. Now shoo, dinner won't make itself.'

Feeling her eyes on your back as you leave. Stunned, it's as if a noose tightens around your neck.

***

Agitated, hands clenching and unclenching, you pace up and down on the same piece of pavement that twenty-four hours ago was so blissful. You haven't slept.

Where the hell is she? He wants me to call.

A shake of your head.

No. How did he find me? Why now?

So absorbed in your thoughts, you don't realise she's standing beside you with a look of concern on her face. 'You okay?'

'Let's go to the park and I'll tell you.'

Settling on the grass, taking hold of your chin, her eyes search yours. 'What's wrong? Tell me.'

'I'm... my dad, he, umm, he turned up... at, at the house.'

Her eyes glisten. 'How? I mean...' Shaking her head. 'I didn't think he knew where you were.'

He doesn't, didn't. I, I don't...' Running your hands through your hair, realising how close you'd come to seeing him, you don't know what to say. Emotions are running wild in you. 'He spoke to Betty.'

Placing her arm around your waist, she squeezes, murmuring, 'It'll be alright.'

Your shoulders slump because you know that's not true. 'No, it won't.'

'What then? What will you do?'

You don't have an answer, but her face mirrors your grief.

Taking your hand, pressing it against her cheek, 'Tell me about your father?'

'Umm...' *How can I? I don't know him. Where to begin?* Resting your head on her shoulder, you start where you think it began. 'My father didn't really seem to care much about me, even from the age of five, I could never please him.'

'What do you mean, didn't care?'

Sighing, you don't want to go over this, like you have a thousand times in your head, but you owe her an explanation.

She runs her fingers along your cheek. 'Did he hit you?'

The answer is yes, but it's not that simple. You're to blame for it all, or so you feel. Your eyes focus on the pond, its surface ruffled by a slight breeze that creates tiny ripples. No ducks today. Answering her, your voice a million miles away, remembering the forest, the toy helicopters, hesitantly trying to put the past into an order she might understand, 'When I was five, he beat me for taking toys from a shop. He would get angry over everything.'

Hand over her mouth, a tear rolls down her cheek. Her reaction makes you feel it's safe to tell her more. Slipping her hand in yours. 'Is that why you left?'

'It wasn't... I never...' You glance at her. If you stop now, you'll never finish, so you continue. 'I didn't feel I belonged. I know it's an odd thing to say, but that's how I felt. I was happy on my own. I'd rather play in the woods than be at home. There, I always waited for the explosion.'

Squeezing your hand, 'Why didn't they stop you from leaving?'

It's a good question, one you've thought about before. Your cheeks burn recalling him, and with a shake of your head, you stare at your feet. Dragging over the hurt of past years makes you wince.

How to explain?

You don't crave pity. Lip trembling, 'They didn't stop me. He came looking for me once, when I stayed in a men's hostel, so I left there too.'

I'll tell her more another time, and the Vic, maybe.

She gasps. 'That's awful.'

Shaking your head, 'No. Not, not really.'

Her fingers caress your arm. 'So, how'd you end up here? In the house with the others?'

Shrugging, 'A friend of mine wanted to come to Sydney to see his sister. We ended up arguing and he left.' Tensing, remembering the following days, considering the close encounters you'd had, and what to tell her. 'I wanted to stay. I believe I was protected. That sounds strange, hey.'

'Protected? What do you mean? How?'

You think about what you've said and wonder if it's true. 'All these things happened that should have hurt me but didn't. In Africa, I got chased by baboons. If they'd caught me...' Your voice trails away as you think about that day. 'A snake lunged at me and at the last moment got trapped by a rock an inch from my ankle. I survived a car crash.' With a smile, 'Oh, and I've escaped from two Sharpie gangs. And when I needed someone, Kevin came along. So here I am.'

You glance across at her. There's a strange look in her eyes — not disbelief, more concern, as if she thinks you may be crazy.

Perhaps she's right.

'I know it sounds strange, but this might convince you.' You haven't thought about Cohen in a long time. What happened scared the shit out of you, even though you were thousands of miles away. 'In Africa, I had this friend, Cohen.

I played at his house all the time. He had this big pool, and I remember his bathroom, with gold taps. I loved touching them. His birthday was coming up, and he was excited; his dad was going to get something special for him. He said I had to be there, but my parents moved back to England about a month before his birthday. One night, my father came into my bedroom and said, 'They've sent me this from Africa,' waving a cut-out from a newspaper. 'It's about Cohen. It says his father hired a plane for his birthday to take him on a joy flight, but it crashed, killing Cohen and the pilot. Cohen's father watched as it happened.' It felt like he was making a point because I'd kicked up such a fuss about leaving before Cohen's birthday. He dropped it on my bed and left without another word. I'd have been on that plane if we'd stayed.'

Shrugging, 'Maybe I should've been.'

She shook her head but remained silent, hunched over, twisting the grass between her fingers. Then whispered, 'Do you... Do you wanna go back?'

You don't want to answer.

She sniffs, wiping her nose with a tissue that appears from under a shirt sleeve. 'Are you gonna call? Now he knows where you live, he'll come back. Won't he?'

'I guess. Would you come if he wants to see me?'

'Won't he want to see you on your own?'

'Fuck that. Please come.'

'Is he coming back to the house?'

'Shit no.' Taking the crumpled card out of your pocket, offering it to her. 'He left a number on this.'

She turns it over in her hand, as you had. 'There's a room number as well. See?'

Taking it from her fingers, 'Don't matter. I'm not gonna call.'

'There's a phone box over there. You can call now.'

Shaking your head, 'No.'

I can't talk to him. He'll make me go back.

'I don't... I can't, he'll...' 'You can't ignore him. I'll be with you.' She stands, extending her hand. 'C'mon.'

'Can't. Got no money.'

'If you wait any longer, I'll have to go. I've gotta get home and feed me rabbit.'

'What rabbit?'

'Mum and Dad got her for me. I wanted a lamb but they said no and got me a rabbit.'

The park has a desolate feel. Dragging your feet, you head to the phone box, imagining this is how a man going to the gallows feels.

Mary, tugging on your arm, doesn't help your mood.

There's an empty feeling in your stomach as you stare at the chrome and glass phone box, and the orange banner with 'Payphone' on it.

Mary nudges you. 'You can't call him from out here.'

She doesn't flinch from the withering look you give her, instead hands you four twenty-cent coins. They clink in your hand. Grabbing the door handle, the door screeches as it opens.

As you go to step inside, Dolly pulls up in her van, yelling out the window, 'Mary, glad I found you. Your dad wants you home. He's pissed off.'

Mary waves a hand, motioning to Dolly, now crossing the street, to be quiet. 'Graham's dad turned up. He's gotta call him.'

A flicker of hope in your chest. If Mary has to leave, you can avoid calling. A smile on your lips, swiftly wiped away in case Mary notices. In a low voice, 'I can call later. If you gotta go.'

Putting her hands on her hips, shaking her head, 'No. If you want me to meet him, call now. Dolly can wait. Anyway, she loves a bit of gossip.'

Chilly fingers trace their way across your heart, but you know when you're beaten. Cigarette butts litter the floor, a lump of hardened brown shit lies coiled in a corner. A cracked phone earpiece and frayed cable provide hope.

Perhaps it won't work.

Hand shaking, you pick up the receiver.

Mary bangs on the glass, mouthing, *Hurry up*.

Putting the phone against your ear, there's a dial tone, your last hope shrivels and dies. Inserting two twenty-cent coins into the slot, finger trembling, you dial the number on the back of the card.

A polite male voice on the other end says, 'The Menzies. Can I help you?'

'Uh, yes. I'm, uh, room four-two-one please. Oh, sorry, that's four, two, se ... seven?'

'Room four-two-seven. One moment.'

Silence, then a crackle and a click. As you fight the urge to slam the handset down, your father's voice resonates in the earpiece.

***

The door of the phone box clangs shut. The business card is slick with sweat, the remaining coins weighing down your pocket.

Was it only a few hours ago he was here?

Mary rushes over, wrapping her arms around you. 'What did he say? Tell me.'

You push her away. 'Shit, let me breathe.'

Stepping back, 'Sorry.' With an expectant glance, Dolly moves closer, ensuring she doesn't miss a word.

'He wants to meet tonight.'

'Tonight!' Mary's hands flutter like a butterfly's wings.

'Yeah, he's here for one more night. Some conference or something.' Your laugh is brittle. 'He waits until it's convenient.'

Mary grabs your shoulders, a mad look in her eyes that you haven't seen before. 'Stop it. I didn't think you wanted to see him, and now you're angry with him?'

Dolly, unable to contain herself, 'Ooh. This is sooo exciting.'

Mary swivels around. 'Shut up. It's serious.'

'I told him about you. He said you should come.'

'I've gotta ask me mum and dad. I can't...'

Dolly interrupted, 'Speaking of your dad, we betta get going.' Then, turning to you, 'What time do you have to be there?'

'Huh? Oh, six, six-thirty.'

'I can take you in if Mary is going. Where is it?'

'I don't... he's at the Menzies? Do you know it?'

Dolly shrugs. 'I got a *Gregory's*. We'll find it. C'mon, Mary, let's go ask.'

Mary remains still, a slight shake of the head. 'I can't. It's too... my hair, and I've got nuthin' to wear.'

Taking her hand, 'Don't go to any trouble.'

Dolly laughs. 'I'll make you beautiful.'

Mary kisses you and runs after Dolly. The van disappears around the corner. *Why now?*

Reflection: Anger

"The loneliness, anger and sadness arrive in the solitude of the darkness, whispering their torment. The weight of a caregiver's bad behaviour is a heavy burden for a child." — Unknown

Healthy anger allows access to assertiveness, allowing us to express our authenticity appropriately. But the abused child's anger comes from a deeper well of emotional trauma and is explosive when it appears. It's a protective response to the fear, sadness, rejection, abandonment and powerlessness we experienced. Because the anger is repressed, it surfaces as rage, resentment or emotional withdrawal.

I know my wounded inner child is angry. I feel it every day. It erupts when feeling helpless or fearful. It wants to yell and scream that the world is unfair. You may have similar feelings of repressed anger. However, the more repressed our rage, the more likely we are going to have an explosive reaction. Of course, we all react differently in different situations. Our level and extent of childhood abuse vary. But all who have suffered childhood trauma carry this simmering rage. The most likely ways in which our repressed anger will surface are by:

- *Being ignored or dismissed in relationships.*

- *Being rejected or abandoned.*

- *Being criticised or feeling unworthy.*

- *Being forced to meet unrealistic expectations.*

- *Being trapped or feeling powerless.*

If you are experiencing any of these, it's an indication that your repressed anger may be ready to explode.

Adult Reaction: Childish Behaviour

As an adult, have you ever acted immaturely and can't stop? I know I have. Perhaps you lashed out at someone before thinking. Afterwards, did you feel embarrassed? These immature reactions are the result of our repressed anger.

When I was nineteen, I shared a house with Mary. It was her parents' house, and her brother didn't like the arrangement. He broke into the house and took some belongings that weren't his. I was so enraged that I wanted to fight him. I followed him halfway across the state, and we fought when I caught up with him. I broke my thumb and have suffered problems with it ever since. My anger was unable to be contained. I lost all ability to reason with myself or calm down. It's a rage that the wounded inner child fosters. It can also explode towards an innocent party. If, over time, you've had feelings of anger but you push them back down. Then, another trigger occurs, and you're no longer able to contain the rage. Road rage is an example of this. In many cases, the incident is not the reason for the rage, it has been simmering for some time, perhaps even years. Anger is not always physical. Once, a partner suggested that my marriage had broken down due to my lack of communication. My anger was immediate and uncontrollable. I walked away and ended the relationship. I'm ashamed of my behaviour, but I couldn't control it. Even though — or perhaps because — she was right. And, of course, ironically, I couldn't communicate with her.

Small things trigger anger. As a child, I lived in fear because of my parents' constant screaming at each other. As an adult, I now struggle to have calm, reasoned responses if I'm criticised or challenged. I always go on the offensive and become spiteful and aggressive as a defensive mechanism. Replicating learned behaviour from my parents.

Healing Exercise: Forgiveness

We need to control our rage. That is self-evident. Begin by thinking of the times you've had aggressive outbursts at work or home and how you felt afterwards. Write down those moments and what caused the outburst. Look for patterns of behaviour and commit to changing them. Our abuse creates fear, hurt and shame and fuels our rage.

Here is a simple exercise for you to manage your anger. Give it a name. I've named mine 'George.' Whenever I feel my anger growing, I say, 'No, George, we aren't going to get angry. It's okay, let it go.' It breaks the cycle. If we don't, our anger will grow until the inevitable explosion. The act of naming anger brings a sense of control. It's a small win, but a win all the same. Unfortunately, due to our abuse, we feel better in an angry state than we do in a calm and understanding state. That's what we learnt as children. Don't worry, we can change. First, recognise it for what it is: repressed anger. It can dissipate once we identify it and put in place measures to stop the reactions. For a more complete resolution to our anger and rage, undertake the following exercise:

- *Take a slow, deep breath, then let it out.*

- *Take another slow, deep breath, and slowly let it out.*

- *Take one more deep breath and let it out all at once through your mouth.*

- *Now, imagine walking into a room.*

- *This room is divided in half by a massive piece of thick, indestructible glass.*

- *A chair is on the other side of the glass, and a chair is next to you.*

- *Take a seat in your chair.*

- *A person with whom you are angry walks into the room and sits in the opposite chair.*

- *While they are sitting in the chair, they can't leave, interrupt you, or move.*

- *Tell them exactly how you felt when they hurt you and how you feel now.*

- *Have this person then respond as you would like them to.*

- *Then, tell this person anything else you would like to say.*

- *Finally, tell them you forgive them and leave the room.*

You can come back to this room anytime you want if you need to forgive someone else. Forgiveness is a powerful tool; you're freeing yourself from the past and releasing negative energy. Self-reflection is also critical in understanding and managing our anger, it helps us engage with our emotions and experiences. There are many books about anger management. I recommend reading Life Changing Anger Cure by Dr. Mort Orman.

Be gentle with your healing. As we release old feelings of anger, grief, abandonment and rejection, we'll feel the pain and trauma of our memories. Practising daily meditation will help as it's beneficial for building a sense of calm and stability.

Understanding my anger led me to forgive my father. It allowed me to unlock my authentic self. I've been on a journey of confronting my past, allowing me to embrace who I am. What would life feel like if you did the same? It's time to find out.

Chapter Twenty

Silent Rage

Mary arrived, shimmering in a lime-green dress. Her hair wound into a beehive, resembling an ice cream in a cone. You don't vocalise that thought — or how you feel in your cheesecloth shirt, the one you purchased from the salesman. You debated wearing jeans but chose the corduroy flares instead.

'Let's go,' Dolly yells.

You grin, hoping to see Terry, but he's not in the van. 'Where's Terry?' Dolly doesn't reply. Mary tilts her head sideways; her eyes speak volumes.

Hands clasped, you stare out the window as street after street goes by. *Will he insist I go back? What about Mary?*

The van slows to a crawl, inching its way along George Street towards Wynyard and the Menzies Hotel.

Trembling, tightening your hold on Mary's hand. She whispers, 'Tell me more about your father.'

'You hesitate, not sure what to say.

He never showed me any affection or put an arm around me unless it was to threaten me. Lamely, you mutter, 'He doesn't like me,' falling back into silence.

The van comes to a shuddering stop before Mary can ask more questions.

A dead weight presses on your chest. 'Thanks for the lift, Dolly.'

'I can come back and get you. I wanna hear all about it.'

Mary gives her a stern look, you smile. 'We're gonna catch the train.'

The van rattles as it pulls away, leaving a familiar trail of smoke. You chuckle. 'That thing will fall apart one day.'

There's a sniff from behind. Turning around, a man in a red coat, matching pants and spotless white gloves stands with arms folded across his chest. A disapproving sneer on his face. 'Can I help you? Are you lost?' His words, clipped and formal.

You inhale. 'Umm, we're, we're meeting someone.'

He turns on his heel, stalks to the hotel entrance and, taking hold of a brass handle, pulls the door open. 'Welcome to the Menzies.' He doesn't sound like he means it.

The foyer is a gleam of marble and brass. Men in the same uniform as the man outside scurry across the lobby, some pushing trolleys with suitcases stacked two and three high. No one pays attention to you.

Mary pulls on your arm, points towards a sign. 'The lifts are over there. What floor is his room?'

Shrugging, 'I don't know.'

'Didn't you ask?'

'No. We can leave if...'

Mary rolls her eyes. 'Stop it. C'mon, let's find out.'

A man shuffling papers glances up as you approach a marble-topped counter. He lets out an exasperated sigh when Mary asks him what floor room four two seven is on. 'Fourth floor, madam.' He speaks in the same clipped tone as the other man.

You whisper in her ear that the hotel must teach them to speak that way. When she giggles, the man shoots her an irritated look.

The lift doors close with a thud. Mary presses '4' on the brass keypad, then plays with a strand of her hair, twirling it around her fingers — you think she's nervous, too.

The lift jolts to a halt; the doors slide open.

You're facing room four-two-seven, and you glare at it as if it's the problem.

Will he yell at me for all the trouble I've caused?

Raising your hand to knock, you freeze, as if dipped in arctic water. Your heart pounds so hard you think it'll break free from your chest.

I can't do this.

The fear is smothering. You want to drop to your knees and curl up into a ball. Pine scent fills your nose. You see two toy helicopters on the ground. Knees trembling, one leg jerks as if struck. A single tear rolls down your cheek. With a shake of your head:

No.

Mary whispers, 'It's okay.'

For you, it's not. It's an opening into hell. But you have no choice. All you wanted was his love, and you know it's not going to be found behind this door. Terrified you'll have to return, not sure that you'll be able to say no.

Why did he do what he did?

Taking a deep breath, settling your heart, you straighten, then knock.

The door opens immediately, as if he's been waiting behind it. Smiling, he embraces Mary, then takes your hand. His hair, greyer than you remember. His shirtsleeves rolled up, unusual for him — he's careful about his appearance. Stepping aside to let you enter, eyes flit from Mary to you. He fusses around her, pulling a chair out from a small table in front of a blue-curtained window.

Your palms sweat, rubbing them on your thighs leaves a damp patch. There's a coppery taste in the back of your throat. Ice clinks as he pours a glass of water for Mary.

She smiles, lifting the glass, her eyes meet yours over the rim, then she puts it down, a smear of red lipstick around the edge.

Your father, with a tight smile on his face, turns to you.

Is he about to...?

You walk to a restaurant on George Street filled with Spanish-style dark timber furniture; not that you're an expert, but it feels odd. The chairs, covered in embroidered material, take two hands to move. In the centre of the table, a candle sputters, a garland of plastic flowers around it.

A thickset woman bustles over, menus in hand.

Expectation and doubt drown you. Understanding he is using Mary as a buffer between you and him doesn't help. Dinner conversation feels like a light bulb flickering on and off. Disjointed and surreal. He focuses on Mary, asking about her job, Sydney, and her family. He skates around the question of you and her.

The heavy-set woman clears the plates, he leans back, pulling out a packet of Benson & Hedges, lighting up, not offering you one. There's a thoughtful expression on his face.

You tense; anger begins to bubble deep inside.

Is he coming to the question that's hung between us all night?

You've never believed in the saying 'You could cut the air with a knife'. But tonight, it's true. His eyes probe your face. 'Your mum misses you. She'd like you to come back.'

There, he said it. What now?

You hesitate, aware he didn't say home. The anger boils, and you want to scream.

Why didn't you love me?

Instead, you mumble, 'I've... I've got work here.'

The veneer slips, a flash of annoyance on his face. 'You can get a job in Darwin.' With a deep breath, controlling himself, the veneer back, he persists. 'Your mum worries.'

'Um, I... I don't think so.' A small boy, lost, scared, flashes into your mind. You struggle to hold back the tears of that five-year-old. You can't explain the horrible, gut-wrenching feeling that rises in your throat; you want to throw up. One thing you're sure of.

He'll never lay another fuckin' hand on me.

Stammering, 'We, we must go, or... or we'll miss our train.'

'Wait. I'll arrange a taxi.' He hurries away. You imagine he's relieved to remove himself. A man behind the counter nods, picking up a phone.

Mary leans closer. 'It's alright.' Her hand on your leg.

You don't, you can't acknowledge her, simply stare at the candle as it finally sputters out.

You know how it feels.

He comes back at a slower pace. 'The taxi will be about ten minutes.'

Waiting in uncomfortable silence on George Street. A slight drizzle falls, adding to the sombre mood between you and your father. You've nothing more to say to him. All night you searched for the right words, even words with which to have a pleasant conversation, and all you could think of was: *Why?*

'Nice meeting you, Mary,' he says as the taxi arrives, kissing her on the cheek and opening the rear door. He hands you money, holds onto your arm for a moment. 'Don't leave it too long.'

You walk to the other side of the taxi. 'Thanks for dinner.'

As the taxi pulls away, Mary wraps her hand around yours, her nails dig into your palm. Wincing, you breathe a sigh of relief. 'Thank God that's over.'

Mary smiles. 'He's nice.'

You shrug.

She wouldn't understand. How could she?

You remain silent for the rest of the journey, your hands locked together. When the taxi pulls up, you turn to kiss her goodbye. Her make-up is streaked, tears on her cheeks, she splutters, 'What now?'

You forgot how she might be feeling. 'I don't know. I'm not...'

She offers a weak smile, then turns and walks into her house.

***

Betty is waiting when you get home, hands on hips. It's unusual to see her up this late. There are no pleasantries, only a sharp, 'Well?'

'Shit, you scared me... sorry... I uh...'

'How did it go?'

'He liked Mary.'

'And?'

Shaking your head, 'There's Mary.'

It's all you can say as an overwhelming tiredness engulfs you. She snaps, 'Excuses.' Stomping to her room, banging the door closed.

Kevin's also awake, he whispers — his version of a whisper, 'You gonna go?'

Doesn't anyone sleep around here?

You don't answer, removing your clothes and climbing into bed, staring up at the ceiling.

Listening to Kevin's faint snores, gazing at the ceiling, your pulse races.

Go or stay?

Giving up on sleep, you go outside. You have to be sure about any decision you make. History tells you that going home will be a problem.

Leopards don't change their spots.

Even though the time away has changed you, seeing him again brought back the terror. But it also planted a seed of understanding: you can't run and hide forever.

I have to return, if I'm ever going to get over what happened.

The moon peeks from behind the clouds, casting a comfortable glow. You smile, remembering a similar moon on that night with Neal in the lounge room. There's a twinge in your heart, sad that he's gone.

Turning to go back to bed, you know what you have to do.

***

Huddled together in the bus shelter, warding off the chill of late afternoon. Mary shivers, pulling her jacket tighter, wiping a tear from her cheek as another sob racks her body.

The words between you are unspoken, neither wanting to voice your fears. You glance across. Her face seems to have had all the joy sucked out of it. Pressing closer, she trembles and mutters, 'You'll find someone else.'

'I won't go.'

'That's stupid. You have to.'

'Will you come with me?'

'I can't. My mum and dad.' Groaning, 'Damn, here's the bus.'

'There'll be another. Stay. Please.'

Mary smiles. 'That's the third one. I've gotta go soon.'

The bus slows, but Mary absently waves it away. The driver toots the horn as the vehicle gains speed, leaving diesel fumes in its wake.

'Well? Would you?'

Shaking her head, 'I don't know.' She stares after the disappearing bus. 'You and your dad need to sort things out.'

'Shit. I'm not sure about that.'

A sniffle. 'You'll forget about me once you get back, I know it.'

Pulling her closer, 'I won't. I promise.'

***

The morning to leave arrives, and you're surprised at how calm you feel. Pulling on your jeans and T-shirt, you think about how the house gave you a life raft, a feeling of belonging. You think of the things you'll miss and those you won't. Kevin's farting, George's bravado and Terry's whining. But you'll miss the feeling of coming home each evening. With a sigh, you think of what happened — changes that would have been unthinkable twelve months ago.

But can I stay the same in the face of my father?

You go to say goodbye to Betty, who's attacking the contents of a saucepan. She stops, raises an arm, sniffs and wipes her nose. You wait for her to turn around. 'You okay?'

She keeps her back to you. 'I'm fine. A head cold.' She starts stirring again, her body wobbling with each movement.

You begin. 'I, thanks for...'

She interrupts. 'Yes. Take care. I can't say I'll miss the racket you and Kevin made.'

You grin. 'Thanks for everything, and for taking a chance with me.' You swallow. 'I don't know what might've happened, if you...'

She turns around, flushed from the heat of the stove, a smile at the corner of her mouth. 'That first week,' she says, the words catching in her throat, 'When you missed paying rent...' She shakes her head, an unruly strand of hair falling from under her scarf, she turns back to the stove.

Bag in hand, walking down the hallway, nose wrinkling at the odour of mildew. *Strange, I never noticed it before.*

From that first day, you'd ignored the peeling wallpaper, the cobwebs in the corners. Now, with your eyes open, the house has a tired look. Your time here is over.

Sticking your head in Alfie's room, finding him lying on his bed, muttering, you leave him with a wave. You pass Kevin and Des in the hallway. Des looks away, but Kevin grins and shouts, 'Big day.' Punching you on the arm, then you embrace. You said your goodbyes yesterday. George is fast asleep, Steve is nowhere to be seen, and you haven't spotted Terry in days.

And that's it — Betty refused to put anyone in Peter's bed after his death.

A car horn blasts as Betty comes into the hallway. 'They'll break that thing if they're not careful.' She wraps you in her arms. 'There's always a bed. Even if I've gotta throw one of the others out.'

Your lips quiver. 'Tha... Thanks.'

'Go on, or they'll leave without you.' With a peck on the cheek and a pat on your back, she scurries back to the kitchen.

The horn blasts again. Walking out of the front door, you take a final glance over your shoulder at the house.

'Hurry up or you'll miss the plane,' Terry shouts, hanging out of the passenger door.

Mary leans against the rear door. Throwing your arms around her, without a word, you both climb into the back: there are no posters on the roof.

***

Terminal One at Sydney Airport is crowded and confusing. Dolly indicates a line of people and tells you to check your bag. You hand the woman behind the counter your ticket, she stamps it and hands it back. 'Boarding gate eleven, have a pleasant flight.'

Mary pulls on your hand. 'Let's go over here,' pointing to a window overlooking the tarmac, ignoring the comfortable-looking lounge chairs.

You watch a plane rumble towards the terminal, the sun bouncing off its Ansett logo.

Mary's hand tightens in yours; she sniffs.

You feel her heart thumping, the pulsing flowing up your arm. Unable to look at her, you watch two men in yellow overalls rolling a set of stairs towards the now-stationary plane. Once in place, passengers hurry down the steps and into the airport.

A whimper escapes Mary as a voice announces that boarding for Flight 922 to Darwin is now open. She throws her head back and squeezes your hand again, mumbling, 'No.'

People shuffle past, you clutch each other and stare out of the window, lost in your individual pain.

A man fumbles with his briefcase, dropping it with a bang to the floor. A mother pushing a baby carriage stops nearby, brushing back the hair from her tired face.

You study Mary, shoulders slumped. You want to reassure her, to tell her it will be okay, but you don't know that it will. There are no words. Or at least, they all feel like a lie in your head.

She continues to stare straight ahead while tears trickle down her cheeks.

What can I say?

The anonymous voice announces final boarding for Flight 922 to Darwin.

Dolly yells, 'Graham, that's your plane.'

'Don't, don't cry. We'll see each other again.'

She shakes her head. 'I...'

'We will. I'll call. And you've got the address.'

Dolly shouts again. 'C'mon or you'll miss it.'

Mary sobs. 'Go.'

'Not until you stop crying.'

Snuffling, wiping her nose, 'I'm okay. Go.'

You walk towards the boarding gate with a breaking heart.

Dolly hugs you. 'Take care.'

'Thanks. Look after Mary.' She nods, sadness in her eyes.

Terry chuckles. 'Don't get into trouble.'

Smiling, 'If you're not around, I'll be fine.'

Kissing Mary, 'I'll miss you.' She nods, hiding her face in her hands.

Standing in line, there's a young boy squirming in his father's arms, struggling to get free. His father puts him on the floor. In the boy's hand is a toy helicopter, its metal body glinting as it catches the overhead light, rotor blades whirring as the boy runs it along the ground, chortling.

Trembling, thinking of another boy with his father. This father, belt in hand, his face a mask of anger and loathing — not of you but of himself. He can't control himself. It's a demon he doesn't understand.

A muffled voice is shouting, but you can't make it out; you're deep in a tunnel where nothing makes sense.

Mary, mouth moving, a worried look in her eyes, shakes your arm.

With a deep breath, calming yourself, you turn to her.

She mutters, 'What? What's wrong?'

You have nothing to say. The fight has begun, and you think you're ready. Kissing her on the lips, turning away, you stride down the passageway, without a backward glance, head held high.

Reflection: The Authentic Self

"Your only obligation in any lifetime is to be true to yourself."
— Richard Bach

The cost of our abuse is the loss of our childhood. A time when we should have been curious and excited about the world became one of fear and loneliness. As adults, we live in that shadow, filled with fear and loneliness. Although we may not always recognise it.

There are days when the reminders of my childhood are overwhelming. I hid my trauma beneath a smile, quip or self-deprecating remark. But then I remember —

my inner child is me, and I am him. It's a connection that neither time nor pain can change. And I smile because that's all I can do.

Survival has been our default for so long that we've forgotten there's another way to live. It takes resilience and commitment to overcome trauma and build a healthier life. Summon the courage to confront your childhood pain. It's a path to healing within your reach. Healing is complicated and often painful, but it's also liberating. I've outlined how childhood trauma impacted me and how it might impact you. My journey has led me to understand that I wish to help others who struggle with similar trauma. We must fight for our original selves — the creative souls we once were. It's not too late, no matter how many decades have passed.

Adult Reaction: It's Never Too Late

If you're in your twenties or thirties, now is the time to lay the foundation for a life without past wounds. If you are in your fifties or beyond, it's time to release the past for yourself and those who love you. In my sixties, I laid bare the trauma I thought would define me forever. Today, I breathe easier, knowing my emotions are not as volatile as they were. I no longer worry about what people think of me. If I'm generous and kind, that's all I need to be. It's far from where I was a few years ago. Once we balance our emotional selves, we begin to live authentic lives. When that happens, we view the world more compassionately and lovingly. One of the most potent ways to do this is to believe in our goodness. When asked what I've learnt from my journey, I say happiness is not given; we must find it. Once we do, we'll never let it go.

Healing Exercise: Ho'oponopono Prayer

I've shared many tools and exercises to help you begin the healing journey, but many more therapies and self-help tools are available. Professional therapy or counselling is not an option but an essential part of this journey. Consider these: inner child therapy, cognitive behavioural therapy, eye movement desensitisation, reprocessing and hypnotherapy. Engage in self-compassion practice, daily affirmations, meditation or art and play therapy. Join online forums or community groups to share your experience in a supportive environment. My study in Clinical Trauma Hypnotherapy, combined with my lived experience, has given me the knowledge and commitment to help others with inner child trauma. If you'd like to learn more about my work, access free resources or be part of my community, join me at GrahamRobinsonwellness.com

On the resources page, you will find a series of books as recommended reading. The more we understand our trauma and its impact on our body and emotional state, the more likely we will succeed on our healing journey. The healing helps the emotional patterns that have governed our lives to recede. They may never disappear entirely, but they will fade into the background.

I want to leave you with a powerful healing tool. The Ho'oponopono prayer is an ancient Hawaiian practice of forgiveness and healing. It will help when you feel anxious, sad or lonely. Ideally, say the Ho'oponopono prayer every morning before you start your day:

1. I am sorry.

2. Thank you.

3. Forgive me.

4. I love you.

There is no greater freedom than recognising when our inner child is screaming for attention, begging to act out — and we respond with understanding and kindness. Remember, healing ourselves helps heal others.

The End

About the Author

Graham Robinson lives on the North Coast of New South Wales and has three children.

He was born in the United Kingdom, the second of four children. At thirteen, he left home and school. In the 1980s, he began a career in radio as a broadcaster and journalist in commercial radio and then for the Australian Broadcasting Commission. In 2005, he moved to Canberra and joined the Australian Public Service following a two-year stint with the University of Canberra. Graham began to experience his trauma in his fifties and, following therapy, started to understand the depth of damage childhood abuse has on the body and emotions. He now follows a career as a Lived Experience Educator to help men find their true self and heal their anger, sadness and shame. *Shattered Innocence* is a revision of his first book, *Pain, Loss & Desire*. Find out more at *GrahamRobinsonwellness.com*

Acknowledgements

This book would not have been possible without the help and guidance of book coach Paul Smitz and Krystal Hille of Hille House Publishing. Both took on the challenge of getting the best out of me to write this memoir. A special thanks to those who helped me overcome my trauma: Life coach Mary-Anne Quezel and the Australian Chapter of Path Retreats, without whom it would not have been possible to share my story. And most importantly, thank you for reading this book. I believe it will improve your life in some way.

Resources

A Pocket Full of Essence — Mary-Anne Quezel.

Atlas of the Heart — Brené Brown.

Healing The Shame That Binds You — John Bradshaw.

Home Coming: Reclaiming and Championing Your Inner Child — John Bradshaw.

Journey of Souls — Michael Newton, PhD.

Life Changing Anger Cure — Dr. Morton Orman M.D.

The Adverse Childhood Experiences Recovery Workbook — Glenn R. Schiraldi, PhD.

The Body Keeps The Score — Bessel Van Der Kolk.

The Deepest Well: Healing the Long-Term Effects of Childhood Adversity — Dr Nadine Burke Harris.

What Happened to You? — Oprah Winfrey & Dr Bruce Perry.

You Can Heal Your Life — Louise Hay.

www.ingramcontent.com/pod-product-compliance
Lightning Source LLC
Chambersburg PA
CBHW032336300426
44109CB00041B/1068